Navigating the Grant Industry® Handbook

By: Fatimoh Harris
Certified Grant Writer®

Excel Publications
P.O. Box 208
Griffith, Indiana 46319
www.grants4me2.webs.com

Ordering Information:
Quantity sales. Special discounts are available on quantity purchases by nonprofits, educational institutions, foundations, corporations, associations, and others. For details, contact the publisher at the address above.

Orders by U.S. trade bookstores and wholesalers. Please contact Excel Publications at excelservices07@yahoo.com, (219) 810-4039 or visit www.grants4me2.webs.com.

Library of Congress Cataloging-in-Publication Data has been applied for.
Harris, Fatimoh

Navigating the Grant Industry/Fatimoh Harris – 1st ed. p. cm.
ISBN-13: 978-1502860040 ISBN-10:150286004X
1. Grants 2. Grant Administration 3. Proposal Writing Title.
HF0000.A0 A00 2016
299.000 00–dc22 2010999999

First Edition
14 13 12 11 10 / 9 8 7 6 5 4 3 2 1
Printed in the United States of America

Cover Design: Monique Atkins (DR Graphix)
Author Photo: Chicago Stylz Photography

DEDICATION

THANK YOU ALL FOR YOUR SUPPORT AND LET'S GROW OUR WORLD WITH LOVE & PEACE!

This book is dedicated to my God and Savior Jesus Christ, parents, Willie and Martha Harris, my beloved late brothers Timothy L. Jones and Clifton Edwards, my beautiful children Jason, Gwendolyn and Tyrone, family and friends.

Thank you all for your patience, support and believing in the "me" God created.

Special thank you to my talented book team of editors, reviewers and endorsers Dr. Sharron Liggins, Nancy Konopasek, Carolyn Thompson, Essie Reeves and Gwendolyn Freeman.

CONTENTS

INTRODUCTION

How many times have you conducted research in the Grant Industry with results leaving you feeling lost, confused and frustrated because discovering the right paths to meet the needs of your agency were overwhelming? To help reduce the anxieties faced in this tremendously rewarding field, I have written from my experiences and studied solid research to boost your confidence and funding success to accomplish the mission for your agency and communities you serve.

This handbook is structured as an educational guide with explanations and activities to introduce or reinforce your Grant Industry learning experiences. As an experienced Grant Administration® and Nonprofit Administration® Consultant, Instructor, Peer/Grant Reviewer and Certified Grant Writer®, I have selected to write this handbook to provide an in depth, self-paced learning experience for readers. My instructions and activities are not intended to promote the advertised monetary fluff of the Grant Industry, which can confuse and devalue honest philanthropic intentions. My intentions are to give you a clear homeschooled experience to activate your learning senses to understand what is expected of you as a prospective grantee and strengthen your skillset as a grant professional.

When attending a workshop or training from Excel Professional Grant Writing & Nonprofit Services, lessons are taught and reinforced through current industry activities and my books *Starting & Surviving: The Nonprofit Industry Handbook* and *Navigating the Grant Industry® Handbook.*

Chapter 1 Introduction to the Grant Industry

What are Grants?

Grants are contributions donated from a grantor/donor for tax-exempt purposes. Ninety-nine percent of grant funding is allocated for IRS federally-approved nonprofit organizations. The most common tax-exempt organizations serve 501(c)(3) purposes for religious, scientific, and educational organizations as well as for, abused children and animals. More lessons about the Nonprofit Industry and Nonprofit Administration® can be found at my workshops and book, *Starting & Surviving: The Nonprofit Industry Handbook.*

History of Philanthropy

According to the National Philanthropic Trust, the history of philanthropy can be dated as far back as 347 B.C. when Plato sustained his academy through his personal donation after his death. Plato willed his farm to his nephew to resume his teachings for educational purposes that supported students and staff members (nptrust.org/history-of-giving). Another historic contribution is captured in 1815 after the original Library of Congress was destroyed by British invasion. Retired President Thomas

Jefferson donated his elite personal collection of over 6,000 books to re-established the Library of Congress (https://www.loc.gov/about/history-of-the-library). Today, the Library of Congress is the sole research based for Congress, largest library in the world and our nation's oldest federal cultural institution (https://www.loc.gov/about/history-of-the-library).

Despite aggressive economic downturns, Americans are compassionate people who donate to causes we support. In 2013, Giving USA reported Americans contribution's totaled $335.17 billion and contributions increased in 2014 to $358.38 billion with 72% of funding from individual donors (givingusa.org).

Do Grants Have to Be Repaid?

Grants are not loans. Grants do not have to be repaid to the grant maker or donor, but the agency must prove they will be ethically responsible, demonstrate financial accountability and have a sustainable future. Loans require personal credit identification such as social security numbers, some type of down payment and a repayment schedule. Grant application processes do not require your social security number, employment salary, employment history, or any other personal information like a loan application.

If you are asked for personal credit identification or inquiries, you are **not** applying for a grant application, but instead, a loan. Do not be fooled by imposters. Grant procedures do not require any repayment when operating a financially ethical operation. Instances where you might be asked to repay a grant occur when there are financial misappropriation and ethical challenges by your agency. There will be a process and a few conversations with the grant maker about any incident(s) and repayment terms.

The *only* repayment request from grant makers might occur when there have been unethical governance and fraudulent practices by the grantee. Remember, grants are public funding. Grantees charged with these practices will face a reprimand including some or all of the following:

- Prison
- Public scrutiny from the media
- General publics
- Nonprofit status revoked by the IRS
- Grant repayment

Always use a Certified Public Accountant (CPA) or experienced financial officer. Conduct in-house bookkeeping practices daily. In order to avoid misappropriations or ethical issues, attend board meetings regularly, conduct board trainings, and maintain a strong relationship with the finance department, the CPA and nonprofit attorney.

Donor Bill of Rights

PHILANTHROPY is based on voluntary action for the common good. It is a tradition of giving and sharing that is primary to the quality of life. To assure that philanthropy merits the respect and trust of the general public, and that donors and prospective donors can have full confidence in the not-for-profit organizations and causes they are asked to support, we declare that all donors have these rights:

I.   To be informed of the organization's mission, of the way the organization intends to use donated resources, and of its capacity to use donations effectively for their intended purposes.

II.   To be informed of the identity of those serving on the organization's governing board, and to expect the board to exercise prudent judgment in its stewardship responsibilities.

III.   To have access to the organization's most recent financial statements.

IV.   To be assured their gifts will be used for the purposes for which they were given.

V.   To receive appropriate acknowledgement and recognition.

VI.   To be assured that information about their donations is handled with respect and with confidentiality to the extent provided by law.

Donor Bill of Rights (continued)

VII. To expect that all relationships with individuals representing organizations of interest to the donor will be professional in nature.

VIII. To be informed whether those seeking donations are volunteers, employees of the organization or hired solicitors.

IX. To have the opportunity for their names to be deleted from mailing lists that an organization may intend to share.

X. To feel free to ask questions when making a donation and to receive prompt, truthful and forthright answers.

Developed by
- Association of Fund Raising Counsel (AAFRC)
- Association for Healthcare Philanthropy (AHP)
- Advancement and Support of Education (CASE)
- Association of Fundraising Professionals (AFP)

Endorsed by
- Independent Sector
- National Catholic Development Conference (NCDC)
- National Committee on Planned Giving (NCPG)
- Council for Resource Development (CRD)
- United Way of America

Common Grant Industry Terms
More terms can be found in the glossary of this book

Allocate – a common industry term that means *to distribute*

Activities – refers to actions and/or tasks occurring within program(s) and operationally

Beneficiary – d*onee* or *grantee* receiving funds from the grant maker/donor

Brick and Mortar – a capital funding term used for remodeling and construction

Capacity Building – Fundable assistance for operational or management purposes. It can also include assistance for fundraising, budgeting, grant/technical writing, financial planning, strategic planning, program planning, board development, training, legal advice, marketing, consulting and other management needs.

Challenge Grants – Funds that stimulate support from other donors because they are contributed only when the grantee is able to raise funds from other source(s). The efforts of the nonprofit to raise money on their own from a broad base of sources such as raffles, banquets, and other creative ventures.

Cost Sharing – portion of cost shared by the agency partners for the purpose of achieving a common goal

Direct Cost – direct expenses specifically related to program/services/projects such as staff, equipment and curriculum

Donor Bill of Rights – The Association of Fundraising Professionals (AFP) guidelines for donors that demonstrate ethical operational practices of nonprofits.

Donor/Funder/Grant Maker – The individual or organization that donates the grant or contribution.

E-Grant - online electronic grant application

Endowment - permanent funds invested into nonprofits to provide continued income support

Fiduciary or Fiscal Agent – lead agency responsible for managing a grant reward of a partnership or collaboration

Goals – Goals describe what the project/program intends to accomplish. It can be a general statement.

Grant Administration® – also referred to as the duties of the Development Administration/Department, describes the summary of work performed to successfully meet the funding needs of a nonprofit and/or for-profit business applying for grant support. The Grant Administration® team processes applications, completes paperwork, provides grant management and perform duties to maintain or increase sustainable funding for nonprofits and/or for-profit entities.

Grant Consultant – a professional contracted to provide consulting services in Grant Administration® duties

In-Direct Cost - cost that support general or administrative operations

In-Kind Contributions – contributions such as equipment, products, professional and labor volunteers, meeting space, or other property received instead of cash donations

Intangible Property - assets of stocks, trademarks, patents, copyrights and goodwill

Objectives - Objectives show what will be changed or learned during activities using measurable outcomes.

Operating Cost – the entire budgeted cost of operating a nonprofit or for-profit business

Operating Income – income an agency or business generate without grants or donations

Performance Goals - relates to objectives being specific, measurable, achievable, realistic and time related (S.M.A.R.T.)

Planned Gifts – a gift that involves a lifetime giving plan from estate and personal contributions

Program – occur ongoing or on a continuous schedule such as an after school program held throughout the school year

Program Cost – cost associated with operating a program

Program Income – gross income from program activities

Project - A project does not occur on an on-going schedule. A project can be an annual event like a back to school event.

Real Property – permanent property that cannot be moved such as land

Request for Proposal (rfp) - A notification of funding available from a grant maker for new or existing grants.

Rubric – A guideline used by peer/grant reviewers to score proposals. It indicates how closely agency applicants followed directions of the rfp to complete the proposal, application and the alignment with funding requirements.

Seed Money – start-up or expansion capital used for operating cost

Sustainability Plan – A written plan that describes strategies to sustain the agency future existence beyond grants and should include income based strategies.

Technical Assistance/Capacity Building – Fundable assistance for operational or management purposes. It can also include assistance for fundraising, budgeting, grant/technical writing, financial planning, strategic planning, program planning, board development, training, legal advice, marketing, consulting and other management needs.

ACTIVITY - Test Your Knowledge

1. What is the definition of a grant?

   _____

   _____

   _____

   _____

2. Do grants have to be repaid? If so, why or why not?

   _____

   _____

   _____

   _____

3. Is a social security number ever needed in the grant or nonprofit processes? If so, when?

   _____

   _____

   _____

Match the following Grant Industry terms.
Look up the terms using the glossary found in the back of this book.

1. Donor/Funder/Grant Maker ____

a. Contributions of equipment, products, professional and labor volunteers, meeting space, or other property instead of cash donations

2. Challenge Grants ___

b. Permanent funds invested to nonprofits to provide continued income support.

3. Beneficiary ___

c. *Donee* or *grantee* receiving funds from the grantor. Both society and the grantee benefits.

4. In-Kind Contributions ___

5. Program Cost ___

d. Funds that stimulate support from other donors because they are contributed only when the grantee is able to raise funds from other source(s). The efforts of the nonprofit to raise money on their own from a broad base of sources such as raffles, banquets, and other creative ventures.

6. Endowment ___

7. Fiduciary or Fiscal Agent ___

e. The individual or organization that donates the grant/contribution.

f. Lead agency responsible for managing a grant reward of a partnership or collaboration

8. RFP (Request For Proposal) ___

g. A notification of funding available from a grant maker.

9. Technical Assistance ___

h. Cost associated with operating a program

10. Seed Money ___

i. Start-up or expansion capital such as a funding request for operating cost.

j. Assistance for operational or management purposes. It can also include assistance for fundraising, budgeting, strategic planning, program planning, legal advice, consulting and other management needs.

True or False

1. Grants must be repaid according to terms agreed to the funder. _____

2. Up-to-date, relevant statistics and information to support service needs should be used for proposals. _____

3. The application process may require your social security number and asset collateral. _____

4. It is a donor's right to be assured that information about their donations is handled with respect and confidentiality to the extent provided by law. _____

5. All rfp applications require an attachment, such as pictures and letters of recommendations to be included with the proposal request. ____

6. A letter of interest allows the opportunity to also send the entire proposal to the grantor. _____

7. A donor does not have the right to have access to an organization's most recent financial statements. _____

8. Grant writers should not be paid unless funding is approved. _____

Chapter 2 Research Techniques, Finding Funding and Resources

Identifying Funding Prospects

Grants procedures take PRAYER, patience, courage, planning, skill, perseverance, motivation, and experience. The key to finding money involves strategic planning, a lot of patience and research. This is an area board members should highly consider as they create a development department and identify a funding researcher in their operational sustainability plans.

Before sitting in front of a computer screen to enter "grant funding" in the search engine or randomly choosing to thumb through a stack of foundation books, it is strongly suggested that you try the practical time and cost-reduction strategies included in this chapter.

Let's begin with the basics of organizing funding prospects. Because your agency may have many funding/cost needs for administration and capital for start-up, equipment and curriculum cost, it is best to structure your funding approach. Of course, funding requests may be easier when the opportunity to request discretionary funding verses restricted funding presents itself. However, grant makers are constantly changing their guidelines, especially those from foundations. Identifying funding prospects comprise of the following criteria:

23

- Selecting the funding type (federal, state, local business donors and foundations)
- Your agency's time table to continue or start services
- Grant maker's RFP process
- Grant maker's response time
- The time it will take the agency to prepare for the RFP process and write an effective proposal

Following other tips and strategies from this chapter will help reduce time in your funding search practices.

Organizing Time and Planning Your Search

To organize time and plan your search, save time by having an outline prepared from your funding and operating strategy plans. Utilizing time management skills is a must for constructive research techniques. The collection of information will support each section of the proposal.

Use the following planning techniques

1. **Decide how much time you want to spend on research.** Don't allow yourself to become frustrated. Schedule your search, for example, 3 hours, 1x per week, etc.

2. **Know the agency service industry and learn Nonprofit/Grant Industry language** by using the glossary terms in the back of this book and the terms found in *Starting & Surviving: The Nonprofit Industry Handbook.* See the following example:

Example Service Industry: Low-Income Seniors

• Define your agency's description of "at-risk." The at-risk term has many areas that relate to its terminology. Don't confuse funders or be too vague when describing your agency's area(s) of interest.

• How will your agency serve low-income/at-risk seniors?

• What are their immediate needs or what identifies them as low income/at-risk?

• What community will you target?

• In your targeted community, who currently serves seniors? (Don't be afraid of competition.)

• What programs do they provide that are different or identical to those of your agency?

• Is there an opportunity to partner? (Eliminate the silo and solo mindset!) We use silo/solo terms to describe when agencies attempt to resolve/reduce community problems *independently* instead of using collaborations/partnerships efforts. The impact is always greater when working together with other community partners.

• How can the agency collaborate with local senior agencies or facilities? Collaborations build funding opportunities. More about collaborations and sustainable plans can be found in *Starting & Surviving: The Nonprofit Industry Handbook* and our workshops.

• What other communities are in need that your programs/services can assist?

3. **Know the operating budget amount.** How much will your agency need to start up or expand? How much is needed for the year? How can you legitimately research what you need without knowing how much you need? Please, do not guess! Create a detailed budget. Be realistic. If this nonprofit is a new endeavor, don't quit your job today expecting to

be fully funded automatically because of your passion or mission to help others.

Each department budget will have revenues and expenses that contribute to the full year operating budget. Include in-kind contributions as a line item. In-kind contributions are referred to as free contributions that eliminates an agency expense. For example, professional services from a skilled nurse that volunteers in his/her nursing skillset and donated equipment are in-kind contributions. In-kind cost must be recorded in both expense and revenue sections on the budget. Be prepared to do a lot of volunteering during the agency's humble beginnings.

Ask yourself, "How much will the program/project cost?" List everything associated with a budget for each program including resources needed for operational cost. Administrative cost plus the program cost equals the total operating cost. Sometimes cost include in-direct cost from administration. For example, in-direct administrative cost may be added from the agency director providing specific program outreach duties. The cost can be in-directly associated to the success of a specific program. Be prepared to justify cost through budget narrations that explain why the cost imposed is necessary. A budget sample is in the appendix.

Narrations are common for grant budgets. Remember, programs are on-going activities. Projects/events can vary from one day, one week or one month.

- *Program* Examples: Youth Sports, Senior Services, After-School Program

- *Project* Examples: Back to School Event, AIDS Awareness Day, Bullying Prevention Month

4. **Find community, state and national industry facts/statistics by using library and Internet resources.** Contact local city, state and local nonprofit agencies that currently serve your industry to develop partnerships to better serve your clients. This information will be used to support the need statement. Some data sites are included in this chapter.

5. **Conduct regular meetings with board and staff members to stay within the focus of the fundings being requested.** Irregular team efforts will cause chaos and confusion that can be illustrated in the proposal writings. This will lead to denied funding. Funding plans, operational plans and preparation should be a *team effort*.

If you do not carefully plan your processes, you can make the mistake of taking too much quality time away from other resources, such as administration duties and personal time. Strategy planning is a MUST!

Finding Funding that FIT Your Agency

Finding funding that *fits* your agency is determined by the development team that has an understanding of the goals and purposes established by the board of directors, investors and staff members. To pursue the agency's funding needs, decide based on the amount needed if your search will be conducted through foundations, local donor solicitations or state/federal departments. Some proposal processes can be lengthy even for small grant requests. They do not have identical preparation processes. Read RFP's and decide which request process is worth your time. It is possible to seek resources from all funding variations.

Sometimes, you will find funding for both programs and projects while researching. STAY FOCUSED and take notes on what and where you have found other funding information for possible future references. It is easy to become curious discovering new data, which is genuinely needed, however, this new data can also be a distraction from your current search mission.

To reduce search time, register for RFP/RFA grant announcements from government, local and internet data services, such as Foundation Center or the U.S. Administration of Children and Family Services. A list of grant data and grant maker resources can be found in the appendix.

Before soliciting for donations, follow these steps:

1. Complete the operating and program budget(s).
2. Be prepared to explain to prospective grant makers the purpose of the request and agency mission.
3. Create a script of talking points that will be communicated through every board member and stakeholder involved in the governance and funding processes. Talking points are discussed further later in this chapter.

Keep in mind that most sites that provide a collection of grant maker data designed to help reduce grant research time will usually charge for services.

The following tips explain how to use grant-making sites and services.

• *Internet search engines* are used for general funding searches. They often display many services that will charge to register for grant announcements and often provide material that can be sought from some free sites. Enroll into free email grant notification registries from foundations, government departments and nonprofit news portals, such as *The Nonprofit Times* (thenonprofittimes.com) and *The Center for Effective Nonprofits* (thecen.org), to gain access of up-to-date industry information and funding opportunities.

Foundation searches can be found online, in foundation books, and/or directly from their websites. Foundations are created through individual/family trust funds, memorials, community nonprofits and for-profit corporations. Foundations from individuals/families, memorials and some companies may require a pre-selected grant request process.

To find detailed information about the process to request grants from foundations, refer to The Foundation Center data base (foundationcenter.org), your local Donor's Forum Library or The Foundation Center books at the reference desk of your local library. The Foundation Center books, The Foundation Center website and Donor's Forums provide local, national and international giving interests; website information, total assets listings, proposal deadlines, board review dates, giving guidelines, and can include a sample of past agencies the foundation has supported. There are grant resources that support practically every cause through foundations.

• **Government** search engines vary but provide grants available within your state and local government departments and through federal departments. Government searches help locate grants, such as community development block grants, sub-grantee opportunities and government departments that donate and are willing to partner with the mission of your nonprofit. Every year, grants are allocated from U.S. Federal Departments to city and state government agencies to strengthen and maintain human service needs.

These grants are distributed by the federal departments to states to provide services and programs within each state. Through many of these government opportunities, departments solicit partnerships with agencies to actually perform the services and provide programs.

Contact or research the website of your local mayor's office, departments of commerce, justice, human services, redevelopment and others for more information about their application process and check the resources in the appendix. Whenever a grant deadline has passed, request the previous application copy to prepare for the next funding round.

They are often found online. The example below can be found on the website of the Illinois Department of Commerce regarding the Community Services Block Grant Program (CSBG). It explains the program's purpose and goals. The appendix also lists the United States departments that allocate grants and some government Internet resources.

Example: Illinois Department of Commerce, Community Services Block Grant Program (CSBG)

"The Community Services Block Grant (CSBG) program was created by the federal Omnibus Budget Reconciliation Act of 1981. The CSBG program is designed to provide a range of services which assist low-income people to attain skills, knowledge and motivation necessary to achieve self-sufficiency. The program also may provide low-income people immediate life necessities such as food, shelter, medicine, etc.

The Illinois Department of Commerce and Economic Opportunity (DCEO) administers the CSBG program in accordance with federal law and the Illinois Economic Opportunity Act. In its administration, the department places an equal emphasis on self-sufficiency efforts and providing relief for the immediate needs of low-income people. The state receives approximately $30 million annually in CSBG funding to provide employment, education, housing and emergency services to the eligible population."
Source:
http://www.illinois.gov/dceo/communityservices/housinga ssistance/CSBG/Pages/default.aspx

4. ***Donor solicitations from local businesses*** within your community and city that are not associated with foundations or an RFP process will also give cash and in-kind contributions to support your agency. Contacting them may merely involve a visit to the manager's office or phone call informing them of your agency's mission and service/program goals. Remember to stay in alignment with your agency's talking points. When businesses agree to donate, they usually always require a letter of interest and proof of the agency's 501(c)(3) status. Your agency should only request donations and grants after receiving IRS 501(c)(3) tax exemption. A pending 501(c)(3) status will not guarantee IRS or grant maker's approval.

5. ***Hire a professional Nonprofit Consultant/Grant Writer.*** (fees apply)
Hiring an experienced professional nonprofit consultant/grant writer will save the agency time throughout the grant and proposal process. Professional consultants work with the board of directors and key staff members to fill the duties of the development department. It is unethical to hire/contract a grant writer based on contingent contracts. Grant writers should be hired based on project cost, as a salaried employee or at an hourly contractor's rate. Excel Professional Grant Writing & Nonprofit Services offer affordable rates, discounts, flexible payment plans and sales. Contact Excel Professional Grant Writing & Nonprofit Services today at 219-810-4039 or excelservices07@yahoo.com to assist with your agency's grant and administrative needs. A full list of services can be found in the appendix.

Fundraising Tips and Strategies

Every business needs a marketing plan. Marketing plans help highlight strategies that help businesses survive. The key component to survival is **income**. Nonprofits, however, have greater soliciting leverages than for-profits through fundraisers. Fundraisers for nonprofits are an income stream for revenue that benefits both the donor and the agency because all contributions are tax-deductible if the agency has an IRS 501(c) (3) determination. A fundraising plan should be included in the yearly operating strategies. Grant makers require nonprofits to raise their own monies to assist with the agency's own sustainability plans.

Instead of waiting until the final weeks of the year or until after your previous fundraising event is over to review up-coming operating needs, change how your agency has structured their fundraising processes. Any day can be your agency's new year's resolution--the day you want to start something fresh. Your board has to purposely make changes and be consistent and accountable to the services your agency provides. This includes having a solid fundraising plan. The fundraising plan should be visited at least quarterly to ensure the agency is following the strategies to meet its fundraising goals.

Having a fundraising plan in place avoids the urgent run-arounds and unnecessary team pressures caused by holding unorganized, last-minute fundraising projects due to diminished or low cash flow to operate services.

Below are strategies for a fundraising plan to help guide your agency into a healthier fundraising process.

• Check with your state's attorney general's office to see if the agency has to register with them to solicit funds. Some states require a charitable solicitation application process to be completed.

• The board, financial manager, development team and executive director should be involved in the planning and execution of fundraising activities. Hiring an experienced fundraising consultant will cost the agency extra money that can be used for programs and services. Only hire a consultant if it is voted absolutely necessary by the board and be prepared to pay consultants upfront.

• Based on the fundraisers from last year, decide what fundraising objectives your agency can realistically achieve during the year. Objectives should be S.M.A.R.T.: Specific, Measurable, Achievable, Results-oriented and Time-based

- The objectives answer the following questions:
  - ○ What is the purpose for the fundraiser?
  - ○ Does the fundraiser relate to our agency's mission?
- How much will the activities involved in the fundraiser cost?
  - ○ Use various marketing styles such as social media, direct mail and tele-marketing. Always have a donation button on the agency's website. How can you reach your audience?
- Use management timelines to effectively execute fundraising plans. Include the small timeline stipulations for soliciting venues, speakers, sponsors, etc. that lead to the main fundraiser activity. These are the paths that will lead to fundraising success.
- Implement strategies for the agency 3 to 5-year fundraising plans.

Other Types of Fundraising

Annual Campaigns are conducted annually/once a year. They are common for solicitations for programs and operating support.

Major Gifts are also called planned gifts and a part of capital campaigns. An examples of a major gift may be $100,000 for a $1,000,000 campaign. Gifts are based on the donor's ability or willingness to support the gift's purpose. Based on your agency grant and donor history, if the agency is a small or new agency, *"the ask"* should be smaller, suggestively, in the range of $5,000 to $50,000. Many times, donors want to analyze the history of an agency's experience of handling annual/large donations before they contribute to small or new agencies.

Capital Campaigns are campaigns that help raise funds for start-up cost and long-term capital cost such as support for the agency's location(s) and service/program expansions. Because this campaign may be one of the longest run solicitations, consider making appealing marketing products such as a brochure of the plan with the vision illustrated in the form of a blueprint or diagram of the building project and a list of goals to complete the plans.

Online Campaigns are solicited through social media networks such as Twitter, Facebook, mass email distributions, and other web-based outlets that have the potential to reach donors from across the world.

In-Kind Gifts

In-kind gifts are a donation of goods or services rather than cash or appreciated property. For example, corporations and foundations may donate computers, office furniture, technical assistance, etc. that has cash value contributed for free. Volunteer time is also an in-kind contribution.

The rate of volunteer labor is currently $22.50 per hour and a professional volunteer's rate is at the marketable cost plus fringe benefits according to 2012 Independent Sector Reports. In-kind products and services are a great way to reduce expenses, leverage cost and show grant makers the commitment of those who believe in the mission of the agency. Remember to include the volunteer hourly rate and the number of volunteers in the budget.

In-kind contributions are budget revenues. This is because your agency will not use cash to acquire them. However, the in-kind cost should also be included in the expense section of the budget.

Budget instruction is detailed in the appendix and *Starting & Surviving: The Nonprofit Industry Handbook.*

More resources, industry definitions, research tips and grant makers info are in the appendix.

Talking Points - Preparing for "The Ask"

All campaigns should start by building relationships with potential contributors. When planning solicitations, put together a list of talking points (a written script) that every solicitor for the agency has rehearsed, using the same language listed to appeal to donors. Rehearse the script with those participating in appealing to potential donors.

Talking points consist of relaying the message of the agency mission and the program/service for the solicitation to the potential donor. It should include interesting details and a relevant message that target the donor. Talking points answer the who, what, when, where and why questions for donors. Here are some steps to cover during preparation.

- Know the amount the agency will request.
- Include board members, key staff, businesses and influential people to participate in the agency solicitation request.
- Send campaign material to the targeted donors.
- Communicate past and current agency accomplishments and prove service impact.
- Be prepared to answer questions. Practice answering questions the donor may ask amongst each other such as program methods, assessments, how giving will benefit/aligns with the donor cause and agency needs, targeted location, etc.

• Set up and confirm the donor/grant maker meeting for the opportunity to *ask* for the donation.

• Prepare *thank you* correspondence no matter the result and send after the meeting.

Don't forget to Say *THANK YOU*

Saying thank you seems like it would be an automatic response, but other than a verbal *thank you*, find other ways to thank your donors and those who couldn't contribute at your time of need. There are many ways to publically announce donor participation such as newsletter/newspaper publications, recognition during a public event, banners/plaques displayed at the agency location(s) and other ways your board decides to celebrate the gift publically. Also, respect donors who wish not to be honored publicly.

ACTIVITY - Test Your Knowledge

True or False

1. All RFP processes are identical. _____
2. It is fine to request donations during the 501(c)(3) pending status. _____
3. All agency stakeholders should have different talking points to build donor interest. ___
4. Some states require a charitable solicitation application process to be completed. ___
5. In-kind gifts are a donation of goods or services rather than cash or appreciated property. ___
6. Major gifts are a part of capital campaigns. ___
7. Online Campaigns are solicited through social media networks. ___

List three search tips that help discover your agency service needs.

- _____
  _____
  _____

- _____
  _____
  _____

- _____
  _____
  _____

List five resources found from researching foundation books and website from the appendix.

1. _____
2. _____
3. _____
4. _____
5. _____

Match the following Grant Industry terms and websites.

Look up the terms using the glossary found in the back of this book.

1. Foundationcenter.org __

2. Program Income ___

3. Grant Administration® ___

4. Grants.gov ___

5. Major Gifts ___

6. Capacity Building ___

7. Giftsandkind.org ___

8. Allocate ___

9. Hhs.gov/FBCI/tools & resources ___

10. Intangible Property ___

11. Goals ___

a. Nonprofit organizations receive access to donated products and special pricing programs

b. Describe what your project/program intends to accomplish. It can be a general statement.

c. Gross income from program activities

d. Planned gifts and a part of capital campaigns

e. RFP notifications and industry information

f. Assets of stocks, trademarks, patents, copyrights and goodwill

g. Assistance for operational or management purposes. It can also include assistance for fundraising, budgeting, financial planning, strategic planning, program planning, legal advice, marketing, consulting and other management needs.

h. White House site of resources that have been assembled to enhance the work of faith-based and community organizations

i. The summary of duties performed by the development department to successfully meet grant funding needs for the agency.

j. a common industry term that means *to distribute*

k. Grant information for more than 900 grant programs

List three fundraising strategies that can be used for your nonprofit.

- _____
  _____

- _____
  _____

- _____
  _____

Complete the following:

Your state may require the agency to register with the _____ _____ office to solicit charitable contributions.

Chapter 3   Logic Models

Logic models are diagrams that help illustrate the beginning-to-end theories and assumptions for operations, activities and resources to deliver services. They are best used as management learning tools to help identify the effectiveness of outcomes/results and are used for evaluation purposes. Logic models may be no longer than two pages and clearly understood by the reader.   A sample logic model can be found in the appendix.

The content of logic models consists of two phases, the agency's planned work and the agency's intended results. The work plans consist of processes and inputs. The agency's intended results consist of outputs and outcomes. A logic model is used to answer questions such as, "What is the purpose of this plan, and what is the agency trying to achieve?" Definitions and examples of this content are described here.

Planned Work:
- **Processes** are *methods, activities* and *strategies* about program objectives and the analysis of its accomplished results.

    Process examples: incorporate nonprofit, sustainability plans

- **Inputs** are *resources* the agency needs to operate.

  Input examples: people, money, equipment, facilities, supplies, ideas, time, attend Excel Professional Grant Writing & Nonprofit Services trainings, etc.

Intended Results:

- **Outputs** are *products* and *services* delivered by the programs/services.

  Output examples: food pantry, senior recreations, youth mentoring

- **Outcomes** include *short-term* and *long-term* results expected after clients are served by the agency.

  Outcome examples: 75% of youth will improve one letter grade by next semester, 80% of parents will gain new parenting skills, etc.

- **Impact** defines how your agency improved administratively, within the communities served, and strategic processes over time and at the end of funding and operating periods. Evaluations of the agency's impact will show positive impact and areas needing improvement.

  Impact examples: The agency impact after five years of service in the Englewood Community will reduce....

  o Example of short-term impact: 1 to 3 years
  o Example of long-term impact: 7 to 10 years

Logic Model diagram can be found in appendix

ACTIVITY - Test Your Knowledge

1. Money, training, supplies and time are examples of _____.

2. Logic models are best used to help identify the effectiveness of _____/results and are used for _____ purposes.

3. List three examples of your agency outputs:

   _____, _____, _____

4. Sustainability planning is an example of the agency _____ _____.

5. Purchasing equipment and supplies is an example of the agency _____.

6. Short and long-term goals is an example of the agency _____.

7. The content of logic models consists of two phases, the agency's _____ _____ and the _____ _____.

8. Work plans consist of _____ and _____.

9. The agency's intended results consist of _____ and _____.

10. Describe two processes your agency will conduct.

1. _____

_____

_____

_____

_____

2. _____

_____

_____

_____

_____

Chapter 4   The Cover Letter and LOI
Descriptions

LOI Agency Introduction

Foundations and corporate grant makers are most popularly known to request letters before entering the full proposal process. Letters of request are identified as cover letter, letters of intent, inquiry, interest or proposal, all commonly referred to with the acronym LOI. The LOI is the first introduction of your agency to foundations and corporate grant makers for partnership opportunity. This outlines the agency history, agency mission, funding request, and shares the opportunity to meet the same need as the grant maker. Follow the grant maker's guide of questions to complete the cover letter and LOI. The various LOIs are described in this chapter.

Cover Letters

Cover letters may be used in the same format dialogue as LOIs explained in this chapter. However, some cover letters may consists of a one page format similar to the sample found in the appendix. Cover letters may also be used in government application processes.

Fatimoh Harris

Letter of Intent

Many times, grant makers request a letter of intent to help grant makers prepare for the number of funding requests to expect from agencies. A letter of intent in the Nonprofit Industry may or may not outline the terms the same as a for-profit letter of intent. For example, the letter of intent can be a simple one-page form requesting information such as the agency name, location, mission, purpose for the request and how many clients the request affects.

Letter of Inquiry/Letter of Interest

The terms for letter of inquiry and letter of interest (LOI) are often crossed, but they have the same definition and both are commonly referred to in acronym format as LOI. The letter of inquiry/interest is the initial contact for many grant makers. It is a brief letter to introduce the agency, describe the nonprofit activities, and inform the grant maker about the grant dollar request. The LOI helps the grant maker decide if a full proposal will be required according the matching interest of the grant maker and requesting agency.

Letter of Proposal (Mini-Grant)

When grant makers request LOIs to be three or more pages, it is often called a letter of proposal. Many foundations use the letter of proposal as their full proposal. You may hear grant writers refer to the letter of proposal as the mini-grant process. For-profit businesses your agency approach for donations, especially for small donations, may ask for a letter of proposal to be submitted with proof of your agency

IRS 501(c)(3) status. Remember to ask community for-profit businesses for donations and partnership opportunities.

LOI Submission Checklist

The paragraph body of every version of the three LOI formats discussed should include the following on your agency letterhead:

1. Introduce your agency name.
2. Direct the conversation to the grant maker in name.
3. Request an amount.
   Specify support type (i.e. program, general operations, in-kind, project, capital).
4. Specify the grant funding cycle your agency desires to participate.
5. Describe the problem your agency will reduce or resolve with statistical or trending proof the problem exists.*
6. Briefly describe the program/project activities, key program staff, and agency fiscal control accountability.*
7. Briefly introduce the agency board of directors and key executive staff.*
8. Include a budget summary in table or paragraph format listing cost for the direct, in-direct and total program budget.* Do not include the entire operating budget, unless it is requested by the grant maker.
9. Summarize the LOI in a paragraph that includes a request to submit a full proposal and your agency's willingness of transparency to share fiscal/financial/administrative operational documents.

Fatimoh Harris

10. The LOI should always be signed by the board president or executive director if permitted by the grant maker.

All LOI formats should be Times New Roman, 12 point, 1 inch margins, 5 to 7 space indentions, headings on each page, and a maximum of three pages in length. If the grant maker requires a shorter or longer LOI page length, *always follow their instructions.*

*Remember, the LOI is the initial sales pitch and introduction of your agency. In the starred areas, you are persuasively giving the grant maker the "bait" to spark their interest in allowing your agency to submit a full proposal later.

A Sample LOI is in the appendix

ACTIVITY - Test Your Knowledge.

1. List the terms for LOIs.

_____   _____   _____

2. What is a term for a letter of proposal?

_____   _____

3. The most common grant makers for LOI's are
_____ and _____.

True or False

1. Community for-profit businesses do not contribute to nonprofit agencies. _____
2. The problem statement can be excluded from the LOI. _____
3. The entire operating budget should be included in all LOIs. _____
4. The LOI can be signed by the program manager. _____
5. The LOI is the initial sales pitch and introduction of your agency. _____

Match the following Grant Industry terms and websites. Look up the terms using the glossary found in the back of this book.

1. **Evidence Based Program Design** ____
2. **Project** ___
3. **Discretionary Grant** ___
4. **Problem Statement (Need Statement)** ___
5. **Logic Model** ___
6. **Letter of Intent** ___
7. **Letter of Support** ___

a. federal government or foundation competitive grants
b. The process of implementing proven research to program design
c. Annual event or activity
d. A letter that informs grant makers of the agency intent to request funding. This process also helps grant makers prepare for the number of proposals they will receive.
e. A letter written in behalf of an agency from supporting organizations or individuals to funders/grant makers.
f. A theory or assumption process that connect short and long term outcomes with program activities/processes and theoretical assumptions/principles of the program.
g. Presents the facts and evidence that support the need/problem for the project/program in your community/state.

Chapter 5 The RFP
(Request For Proposal) Process

Communicating With Grant Makers

Grant makers are not always accessible for the constant communication that some grant candidates might desire. When funding becomes available from grant makers, it is announced usually 30 to 45 days before the due date. Grant makers provide bidders conferences, meetings and webinars to explain the funding opportunity. This is an opportunity for grant makers to answer questions that potential grantees may have in order to clarify the grant purpose, target population, program interest, and other contents of the request for proposal (rfp) process.

To best prepare for questions to ask at the meetings and during webinars, review the entire rfp with the development department, grant writer, board members and key staff. Then write the questions to be answered during the bidder's sessions. If all your questions are not answered, email unanswered questions to the grant contact person. Do not make uninvited visits to grant makers and call only if it is permitted by the grant maker. Calls are not always welcomed so that interested grant candidates can work on the rfp process with their team.

Unfortunately, grant makers have to be cautious of agencies that try to obtain every response for their application and proposal to try to win favor from the grant officer. This would be an unfair advantage to other grant candidates and create unethical practices for the grant maker.

Types of Grant Applications

There are two types of grant applications-- printable and online. Both applications can be found at the company, foundation, or government agency website along with their funding priorities, deadlines and any information needed to complete the rfp process.

When searching online for grant information, you can usually look for the small print menu category that may read "about us," "corporate responsibility," "foundation" or "capacity building." Funding priorities define the philanthropic interest grant makers seek to fund. If your program/mission interest does not align with the priorities of the grant makers, do not waste your agency's time by trying to convince the grant maker why they should fund your program. Your grant request will not be read or considered. Grant makers invest in their own specific charitable cause(s).

Deadlines may vary according to when grant maker boards meet to review rfp applications. Their variance could be annually, rolling (continuously) or quarterly. To help keep up with the various deadlines of grant makers; it is be best to set up a proposal/grant calendar for grant preparation to organize deadlines. Also, subscribe to a data base that email rfp notifications.

Online applications are commonly referred to as e-grant applications. This type of application must be assessed through the grant maker/funder website. There is usually a pre-screening of qualifying questions to answer before you can begin the application process. Every online grant maker requires the agency 501(c) (3) status to already be approved by the IRS.

Foundation/Corporate applications are transitioning exclusively to online application procedures. There are very few foundations/corporations still using print applications.

Federal applications are directed by grants.gov website. Grants.gov provides very resourceful information for grant requests for states, nonprofits, tribal and for-profit funding interests. The site provides grant information for more than 900 grant programs. In order to qualify for federal funding, make sure your point of contact (POC) follows all registration procedures. Notice of Funding Availability (NOFA) may only have funding available for states. If so, contact the state office and ask how your agency can be included in the application. The appendix includes resources to locate federal departments that participate in funding opportunities. To prepare the agency for future funding, go to federalregister.gov to review current and past funding deadlines from the government. This will help to gage the proposal-planning and grant calendar and should reduce the rush of last-minute proposal preparation.

The White House also provides a specific administration called Office of Faith Based and Neighborhood Partnerships for Community Outreach. The website is located at www.whitehouse.gov/administration/eop/ofbnp. Check your Governor's website for information about the Faith Based and Neighborhood Partnerships in your state.

Depending on the application/proposal complexity, it is always best to begin working on grant proposals 12 months before deadlines are due. This will help to eliminate avoidable mistakes and can reduce stress on your development department and grant writer.

Chapter 8 give tips on how using grant/peer reviewer's rubric notes can help redesign the proposal when a proposal is rejected. The rubric in the appendix illustrate how grant/peer reviewers analyze grant applications. Use these tools to help your proposal processes.

ACTIVITY - Test Your Knowledge

True or False

Communicating with grant makers

1. It is ethical to try to gain an advantage over other agencies by constantly calling the grant maker. ____

2. When possible, visit the grant maker's office to get unanswered questions resolved. __

3. It is best to review the entire rfp with the development department, grant writer, board members and key staff. ____

Grant Applications

1. Grant makers funding priorities define the *interest* your agency seeks to fund. ____
2. All grant maker application deadlines are on rolling basis. ____
3. It is best to begin working on grant proposals 3 months before deadlines are due. ____
4. 501(c) (3) determinations are not required to complete online applications. ____

Fill in the blanks

1. The White House Office of _____ _____ and _____ _____ is a resource for nonprofit agencies.
2. _____ applications can be found on the website grants.gov.
3. In order to include your agency application in a NOFA, your agency should contact your _____ office.
4. _____ _____ define the philanthropic interest grant makers seek to fund.
5. _____ _____ are commonly referred to as e-grant applications.
6. Funding is announced usually 30 to ___ days before the due date.
7. _____ and _____ applications can usually be found at the company, foundation or government agency website.

Chapter 6 Grant Administration® Processes

What is Grant Administration®?

Grant Administration®, also referred to as the duties of the Development Department, describes the summary of work performed to successfully meet the funding needs of a nonprofit and/or for-profit business applying for grant support. The Grant Administration® team processes applications, completes paperwork, provides grant management and perform duties to maintain or increase sustainable funding for nonprofits and/or for-profit entities.

The Development Department is a recognized term for Grant Administration® used in the Grant Industry. However, the term Grant Administration® can be more understood by novice and others unfamiliar with Grant Industry practices because it relates the many components of grant processes. A description of the responsibilities of Grant Administration® duties are outlined here and throughout this book.

Grant Administration® Positions, Procedures and Responsibilities

The **project manager/executive director** gathers program and management concepts from staff and presents them to the board of directors and stakeholders. He/she also assists the executive director or key personnel with the preparation of the operating expenses and programs for future operating plans. Operating plans should be forecasted at least 3 to 5 years. The project manager assists or manages the following tasks:

o Prepare project/program descriptions
o Outlines goals, objectives, tasks and activities
o Coordinates management, staff and volunteer plans
o Evaluates plans and outcomes
o Assists with program(s) and the operating budget
o Prepares grant reports

The **statistics researcher** gathers and keeps records of the following information:

o Demographics of the residents and community the agency serves
o Statistics and records showing progress/strategies that assist clients of the agency
o Statistics about community issues and needs

The **funding researcher** researches all funds available to reach operational and program goals.

Fatimoh Harris

The **office clerk** handles the documentation of the agency. The following documentation will be required for grant processes and should be stored in the agency's files:
- Federal Identification Number
- 501(c) (3) IRS determination letter
- Mission statement
- Agency history
- Organization chart
- Annual report
- Newspaper articles/clippings/testimonials
- Financial statements & 990 IRS filing
- Completed projects list
- Awards, acknowledgments and nominations
- List of board members
- Standard Operating/Policy Procedures
- Annual operating and program budgets

The **draft reviewer** reviews proposal drafts and helps with editing.

The **draft proofreader** checks drafts for content and typographical errors. If an internal source is not available, an external consultant should be hired.

The **grant/proposal writer** gathers input from all sources and works with all development staff members. This person does the following tasks:
- Repetitively reads the request for proposal (RFP) application guidelines
- Prepares and rewrites the draft
- Aligns proposal components with RFP requirements and the rubric
- Sends draft for review and proofreading
- Prints final proposal and attachments

- o Postage or electronically mail proposal
- o Verifies proposal is received from the grant maker
- o Utilizes software such as, Word, Excel, Adobe Reader and/or Power Point

The **community networker** has the main responsibilities of building relationships and communicating with potential donors/grant makers, potential business partners, other prospective collaborating nonprofit agencies, and community officials.

The **chief financial officer** is responsible for engaging board members, stakeholders and key staff in project achievability and all budgets. This person does the following tasks:
- o Prepares annual budgets
- o Manages grant and fiscal agent accounts
- o Prepares or hires a CPA to prepare financial statements
- o Prepares reports for the IRS

Grant Administration® Processes

After meeting with all stakeholders involved in the proposal process, the next step is to continue the Grant Administration® process. This involves *organizing* all the material from your research, logic model, appendixes, and community/outside supporters to ensure the application has the required attachments and that the proposal aligns with the purpose of the funding partnership between your agency and the grant maker.

Only include attachments specified by grant makers with the application and be sure that they are in the order they require. Following specific directions may seem like small mistakes can be overlooked. It is never a good idea to go into the proposal/application preparation process with this mindset. Peer readers and grant makers have big decision-making responsibilities. You do not want to frustrate their process further because your work is unorganized. Do not add any additional material that has not been requested by the grant maker in hopes of improving your agency's advantage for acceptance. Avoid a potential rejection by simply following grant maker's directions.

The steps needed to prepare for engaging grant makers and completing applications and the rfp process are described here. The steps may vary according to grant makers and rfp guidelines.

Grant Preparation Steps

1.   Assemble documentation listed in the office clerk section described earlier. Also, include the previous year CPA audited accounting record.

2.   Provide a list of active board members. Grant makers may want to talk to them. Provide talking points or a script for all key stakeholders.

3.   Prepare a grant and/or donation history. The more grants/donations funded, the better the qualification.

4.   Include the mission/purpose statement.

5.   Outline program/project/organization goals (broken down per program/organization need).

6.   Describe the current and past successes of the program/project/organization outcomes.

7.   Outline the program/project/organization budget (written out with justifications/narrations).

8.   Create talking points for steps 6-9 and 13 for all board members and investors to use to promote the agency services and mission. It should be a 5-7 minute agency sales pitch for donors and grant makers.

9. Provide written/verified testimonies illustrating that the agency has worked for the community and its constituents.

10. Appoint an agency representative as contact person.

11. Describe current partnerships/collaborations with the community, preferably with a working history. Partnerships/collaborations are IMPORTANT. It shows your agency is willing to form a united commitment for the greater good for the public and the agency's mission.

12. Conduct grant and sustainability strategy planning sessions. (This is a MUST for the life of the agency!) Planning sessions discuss the problem(s), need(s) and resolve of your agency interest with the agency team members. Due to the timely and thorough details needed for sustainability and grant planning sessions, these sessions should be separate from organizational strategy planning sessions and the results reported during organizational planning meetings.

13. Provide proven program evaluation and assessment methods.

14. Obtain community support from businesses, other nonprofit agencies, politicians, and community members.

Letter of Support, Partnerships and Collaborations

Some grant processes require a letter of support. A letter of support is similar to an employment reference letter. It justifies the importance of the agency, key stakeholders and provides testimonial value about the agency's services. Common practices for nonprofits required by grant makers are collaborations and partnerships. Grant makers require nonprofits to form partnerships and collaborations because it increases the success of community services. Collaborations and partnerships have a greater capacity to strengthen communities and provide greater impact to the lives connected to these resources. The relationships between the lead nonprofit agency and the collaborators/partners provides the best solution for grant makers to achieve their philanthropic giving interest.

To avoid legal ramifications, mistrust and misappropriations of funding, partnerships and collaborations should have a written memorandum of understanding that describes the mission of each partnering entity, description of partnering activities and roles, as well as financial needs for each party of the collaboration/partnership. Both, letters of support and partnerships/collaborations should exist to support the agency's legitimacy and service purpose before the grant application and proposal processes begin.

Descriptions for the letter of support and memorandum of understanding (MOU) for collaborations/partnerships are provided here.

Letter of Support

A letter of support is a letter written on behalf of an agency from supporting organizations or individuals to funders/grant makers. The supporting organization can be a business executive, a nonprofit organization, government/political representatives, community leaders, other grant makers/donors and/or clients with testimonies about their personal success from the agency.

When seeking a letter of support, the request should be from a representative who is *familiar* with the mission and success of your agency. However, there are times when support from government and community representatives would best support a large collaborative grant request. When seeking acknowledgement from government or community supporters who do not know about your agency, it is best to be respectful of their time and strategize your approach instead of making random, unorganized appeals.

Here are some tips to help your board with the appeal process:

• Before attempting to reach out to potential supporters, discuss the support opportunity and reasons for appeals at the board meeting and vote on the decision to make support appeals.

• Decide who will be the communicator on behalf of the agency at a board meeting. There should be one main contact person and a backup when the main person is not available. For high profile government, community and business leaders, the board president is normally the main communicator.

• Be prepared to explain the reason for the support letter. Be prepared to *justify why* the support letter is necessary.

• Be prepared to explain the project/program/operating funding request. The potential supporter may even ask to meet the board, executive director, and/or key staff; discuss the funding request; do a site visit of the facility; and observe the program. Remember, your agency is asking to use their name and government/community representation to stand with your agency cause.

• Research the potential supporter *interest* using their website, social media and their business office. When government officials run for office, they always have various interests of changes they desire to help within communities, the state and the country. This is also true for community leaders and business philanthropists.

• Use information from your research to compare the interest of your agency with the interest of the potential supporter. Remember, you are looking for interest that will allow your agency to request support for funding from the grant maker that the potential government/community leader and/or business philanthropists also desire to see changed within the community/state/country.

• Align the common interest with a dialogue script, also called talking points that will win the interest of writing a support letter to form a partnership in your agency mission and funding request. The talking points should be practiced among board members, the executive director, key staff and other stakeholders involved in the support request process.

• After the board decides on its strategy to request support, contact the potential supporter and ask what steps the agency need to take to make a request for a support letter. Follow the steps needed to get the support.

• Use the following dialogue for the support letter to ensure your agency obtains the information needed to appeal to grant makers.

Support Letter Dialogue

After the supporter agrees to provide the letter, there should be specific dialogue in the letter that illustrates *support* for your nonprofit agency mission and the funding request.

The letter should attest to the benefit of your agency receiving funding from the grant maker to help serve clients or improve/strengthen agency operations. In other words, the letter supports why the grant maker should support your nonprofit programs/services.

The letter should be written in a very persuasive format that influences the grant maker to contribute to the nonprofit cause. The support letter should answer grant maker questions such as:

• What changes will be made in the community and/or to individuals through services provided by the nonprofit?

• Does the agency have a good community reputation?

• How does this nonprofit differ from others?

• What are the financial procedures of the agency?

- Who is responsible for the fiscal control of the agency and what is his/her experience?

The letter should include the benefits the supporter receives from your agency or state the agency's value in its service area(s). Also, make sure the letter states the length of supporting years and financial or other types of contributions made by the supporter toward agency causes.

If the supporter is a community or collaborating partner, the supporter should indicate how they currently or will work with your agency. The positive effects of the collaboration for clients and the service area(s) should also be indicated.

The suggested page length should be no longer than one page. The letter should be addressed on the supporter's letterhead to the grant maker. It is best to address the grant maker contact person directly. Some support letters are addressed using open salutations such as "to whom it may concern" or "dear sir/madam" are also acceptable. Remember, the support letter should sound enthusiastically positive in introduction of support. For example, "We are pleased to support Harris Foundation for Girls Afterschool proposal to the McAnderson Foundation."

The body of the letter should plead the cause for the need of the grant, including the benefits previously as discussed. An example of a closing statement should return to supporting the agency, for example, "Please help continue the success of the Harris Foundation for Girls Afterschool Program by expanding their services to reach 50 additional disadvantaged girls." Lastly, the format of the letter should be in regular type set such as Arial or Times New Roman, 12 font, one page, single or 1.5 spaces, and signed by the supporter's board president/CEO.

If the president/CEO is from a large company and difficult to reach, the executive director or an executive designee should sign the letter.

Memorandum of Understanding (MOU) for Collaborating Partners

In the Nonprofit Industry, a memorandum of understanding (MOU) is an exchange of services/tangibles formally agreed upon between two or more partners that benefits the community and clients. The memo should address the type of services/tangibles each partner will contribute during the financial and administrative agreement terms and the purpose of the partnership. It should be signed by the partnering board presidents/CEO. There should also be recognition of agreement voted by all agencies involved in each partner board minutes as well as a letter from each board stating their board support for the exchanges of services and partnership. This should be kept on file in case grant makers or other investors request to view it.

Before formally agreeing to the partnership, there should be a clear understanding of how each partner will receive benefits (financial and all other benefits) from the agreement. Options of commitments received from MOU/collaborations can be in areas such as equipment usage, location usage, providing volunteers and staff, financial support or service exchanges.

An example of MOU benefits can be an agreement among an employment agency, child care and women's group home provider to serve homeless women with children. All three partners can request grant funding as a unit in one grant application/proposal to serve the same population of women with children. State if this partnership is a pre-existing arrangement or new partnership that is requesting grant support. The partners can serve in their areas of specialty, state how the collaboration will work and receive an agreed amount of grant funding as needed per partner.

If your partners will participate in the grant being requested, the MOU should state how the collaboration of activities will be managed effectively and which agency has been selected as the fiduciary agent of the grant after rewarded. The MOU should also state how the goals of the partnership align with the goals of the funder and include the collaborator's expertise showing their track records of achievements independently and as partners. This type of union can provide great benefits to the clients they serve.

One of the main interests experienced grant/peer reviewers seek when reading proposals from prospective grantees is their collaboration efforts. Collaborations strengthen and benefit clients greater than an independent *silo* agency and the grant acceptance possibilities are higher.

For more information about budgets, sustainability, capacity building, collaborations, strategy planning and Nonprofit Administration®, attend the series of Nonprofit Administration® Workshops and purchase *Starting & Surviving: The Nonprofit Industry Handbook* by Fatimoh Harris at Amazon, www.grants4me2.webs.com or call 219-810-4039.

ACTIVITY - Test Your Knowledge

True or False

1. A letter of support is *addressed* to the nonprofit. ____

2. It is fine for every board member to express their own individual talking points. ____

3. Collaborations have better opportunities to win the interest of grant makers. ____

4. Letters of support help illustrate *why* the grant maker should support your nonprofit programs. _____

5. The development department conducts Grant Administration® procedures in the Grants Industry. _____

**Match the following Grant Administration®
terms from this chapter**

1. Draft Reviewer
____

a. Gathers and keeps records of the following information: Job details including demographics of the residents and community the agency serves, statistics and records showing progress/strategies that assist clients of the agency, statistics about community issues and needs

2. Project Manager/Executive Director ___

b. Reviews proposal drafts and helps with editing

3. Community Networker ___

c. Gathers input from all sources and works with all development staff members. Job details include: repetitively reads the request for proposal (RFP) application guidelines, prepares and rewrites the draft, aligns proposal components with RFP requirements and the rubric, sends draft for review and proofreading

**4. Statistics
   Researcher**
   ___

**5. Proposal
   Writer** ___

d. Gathers program and management concepts from staff and presents them to the board of directors and stakeholders

e. Builds relationships and communications with potential donors/grant makers, potential business partners, other prospective collaborating nonprofit agencies, and community officials

Chapter 7   Writing The Proposal

The Proposal Breakdown

The information in the proposal is crucial in its deliverance to peer readers and other decision makers. Therefore, it is vitally important as a part of your agency's sustainability process to be clear when explaining the contents within the proposal. This chapter will explain key areas of proposal sections.

Although your agency passion to assist those in need and carry many administrative responsibilities of which clients do not see, it is important to have an experienced grant writer and/or recruit a development team to handle your grant funding procedures.

The entire proposal is actually a series of answers grant makers are seeking about your agency services that will help them find the *best investment* to fulfill their philanthropic interest. Your job is to *propose* providing the best quality of services using *proven researched based methods* to effectively improve or maintain your client's quality of life and deliver the greatest service impact for a community (geographically or specific types of clients) or region served.

The entire proposal process consists of the following sections:

1. COVER LETTER/LETTER OF INTENT (LOI)
2. GRANT APPLICATION
3. EXECUTIVE SUMMARY
4. PROBLEM/NEED STATEMENT
5. PROGRAM DESIGN – Goals, Objectives and Activities/Plans
6. PROGRAM MEASUREMENTS
7. BUDGET
8. APPENDIX
9. REPORTING

*Always follow the instruction of grant makers proposal outline which may differ from above.

The logic model works effectively to help clarify the flow of the program design. Please refer to Chapter 3 to learn review how to create a logic model.

Grant Proposal - A grant proposal is a financial/in-kind request to enter partnership with donors/grant makers for the success of a common philanthropic goal. It narratives a proposed program/service in alignment of the agency's and grant maker's mission.

Funding opportunities are announced by foundations, corporations and government departments through request for proposals (rfp), notice of funding availabilities (nofa), and public announcements (pa).

A grant proposal consists of several sections which are outlined according to the specifications of the grant maker and most requests have deadlines. Completion of proposals should not be a rushed process. The proposal process should be calculated to include at least 12 months before deadlines are due. Preparing months or a year before proposals are due will give your agency time to get the clarity needed for the request and make time for the Grant Administration® to organize the many duties that detail their job.

If the grant/development department consist of one individual or less than five people, then the agency should have a two year proposal calendar to submit proposal plans for future development department duties in order to accomplish all the duties required in chapter six. Hiring a grant writer as a staff member, contracting an experienced grant writer or getting grant/development training may save valuable time and help resolve the frustrations inexperienced staff or volunteers will have figuring out the proposal process. Excel Professional Grant Writing & Nonprofit Services provide Grant Administration® services and have won millions in funding rewards.

The reading of a completed proposal should be a smooth delivery of concepts. In other words, readers and other decision makers should have a clear picture of your agency mission, program and operations by following the proposal flow from the executive summary all the way through the appendix section. This clarity in flow includes information about partnerships/collaborations and community support letters which should further justify the purpose of the request, service benefits and need for your agency services.

Be careful to stick to the subject interest of the grant maker. Straying off into other non-relatable agency issues or situations can become confusing, overwhelming and frustrating to the reader of the proposal. Remember the reader often have several applications to review and your agency want to stay on track by being clear by only discussing what is interesting to the grant maker.

Grant makers are more confident in agencies with a broad base of support. When other donors and members of the community invest in the program, it adds to the legitimacy of the proposal request and value of the program. The proposal should also mention other financial supporters of the program, agency and also discuss the areas in the program design about how the collaboration of partners work efforts will benefit clients and the community. Some sections of the proposal are briefly outlined below.

1) The title page may only consist of a preprinted form consisting of the agency name, agency address, board president contact information, a summary of the request, grant cycle and the request amount. It is usually issued by the grant maker as part of the application.

2) Ninety percent of the time, the letter of intent/inquiry or in some request, cover letter, is requested before a full proposal can be submitted.

3) The executive summary is submitted with the full proposal.

4) The mission statement describes your agency's purpose or reason for existence and aligns with the agency's services provided to clients. Additionally, the executive summary and mission statement *shows the funder* whether there is a match between your agency's goals and the funder's goals.

5) The problem or need statement, with proven statistics and trends, identifies there is an issue in

your target population that can be reduced or resolved through partnership with the funder/grant maker.

Executive Summary

The executive summary may be the most important piece after the submission of the letter of interest/inquiry. This section engages the funder in the excitement of a potential match or signals a warning of a potential denial. The executive summary should *sale* the services your agency work so hard to provide.

The information within the body of an executive summary should include the following:
- Introduction of your agency name
- Direct the conversation to the grant maker in name (ex: The Allen Foundation)
- Tell the request amount needed. *Note: Your budget and proposal narrative should justify the request.*
- Identify the type of support the agency need (ex: program, general operations)
- Inform them of the grant funding cycle the agency is targeting (ex: 2nd quarter)
- Identify the problem(s) your agency will address with statistical or trending **proof** the problem exist. Briefly identify the main problems in the executive summary. There will be opportunity to elaborate in the proposal narrative.
- Briefly describe the program activities and solutions that will help resolve the problem(s).
- The executive summary format is usually Times New Roman 12 point, 1 inch margins, 5-7 space indentions, one page in length. If the grant maker

require a certain format, *always* follow their instructions.

Problem/Need Statement

The problem/need statement explains <u>why</u> your project/program is necessary for the target population the agency serves. To illustrate the problem/need to grant makers, present the *facts* and *evidence* that support the need using statistics, reports and trends from research data. Remember to cite all sources when proving your case. Research sources can be found in the appendix of this book. Discuss the impact your agency will make to the population(s) to be served. Use these facts to support the problem(s) that your agency will address in the proposal narrative and with how your agency will reduce the issues. The data should consist of relevant, relatable circumstances within your local or a specific community, city, state and nationally.

The problem/need statement establishes your agency understanding of the problem in the community *AND* convinces the grant maker that your agency has the qualifications to relieve the needs. The logic model will help illustrate the relief or resolution to the problem.

The statement of need/problem should answer the following questions:

➢ Why is this situation the target area of need for your community or clients?

➢ What difference will your agency make in your community/city by addressing the issue?

➢ What is the purpose for developing the proposal?

➢ Beneficiaries – Who are they? How will they benefit from your services? (short and long term)

➢ What is the nature of the problem?

➢ How did your organization realize the problem(s) exist?

➢ What is currently being done about the problem within your city, through other local community nonprofits and nationally?

➢ What alternatives remain available after funding has been exhausted? In other words, briefly explain your sustainability plans here and more in the narrative.

➢ What will happen to your project/program if the grant maker decides not to fund your agency? Please do not state *"we will not survive"* or tell them your agency will not have money after the grant ends. Your proposal will be *REJECTED*. The agency funding plan should be addressed with the sustainability plan in the proposal.

➢ How will your agency resolve or reduce the problem(s)?

PROGRAM DESIGN:
Goals, Objectives and Program Plan

The program design is where the proposal narrative begins. This narration is where you discuss the program plans about the goals, objectives and tasks to carry out the agency mission. In the Grants Industry, we refer to this process as the "program method or action plan". The program design answers for the grant maker/peer reader the following questions.

➢ What are the program/project plans to accomplish the mission/goals proposed?

➢ How will this donation help address the project/program needs? The program design addresses the activities from the agency that will get the program/project started or maintain current existence.

> ➤ The plans for the program design should use action verbs like *will, execute, initiate, etc.*

> ➤ Tell the time length of activities for operations from the time the agency receive funding to the end of the funding period? This can be diagramed in a table format.

> ➤ The program method, also called the program design, is the step-by-step procedures to carry out the program/project plans to reach the objectives; these actions identifies with the resources needed and required timeline for the success of the services provided.

> ➤ Programs vs. Projects/Events

> o Programs occur on a continuous schedule, for example, during an entire 10-month school year.

> o A project/event does not occur on a continuous daily, weekly or monthly schedule. A project/event can be an annual event like a back to school celebration or health fair.

How can the grant maker help?

Genuinely, the grant maker wants to help resolve or reduce the problems faced by your clients. After the agency services are explained, discuss how the grant maker/funder can contribute financially as a partner. The program design discuss how the relationship with the funder and other collaborators will work together to change the lives of the clients your agency serves.

Fatimoh Harris

What is your plan and how will your programs impact the lives of your clients?

The proposal explain the program(s), operational strategic plans, curriculum, requested amount, assessment and evaluation methods to deliver services. The proposal should also include how the board will contribute to the effectiveness of service outcomes and sustainability strategies *other than grants* such as program income, fundraisers and in-kind contributions to demonstrate future services will exist after the funding period.

When working on operational and program plans with board and stakeholders, use the logic model to help illustrate the agency processes.

Explaining the program design will help grant makers visualize the concepts of the program purpose, program plans and how they will be achieved using goals, objectives, program activities planning, resources and timeline.

Be careful not to confuse in writing the *program design* section with the *problem/need* section. The problem/need section establishes your organization understanding of the problem or need as an existing epidemic within the community or region BUT *the program design* section convinces the grant maker your agency has the qualifications to address the issues by providing structured services to clients. The program design section explains the program(s) your agency will use to help resolve the issues discussed in the problem section.

What resources will be needed to operate services?

The cost of your resources should be included in the budget and discussed in the proposal. The proposal explains why the cost of resources from the budget is needed. Examples of resources are equipment, staff, money, volunteers, supplies, facility, etc. The resources and the purpose for the resources should also be seen on the logic model.

Please note: The steps needed for the program design and other proposal processes discussed in this book are also relatable when soliciting for projects and events.

PROGRAM METHODS:
Goals, Objectives and Tasks

Every proposal should illustrate goals, objectives and tasks relatable to the agency's mission, vision and programs or projects as solicited from grant makers.

To clearly define goals, objectives and tasks, it is best to work with key stakeholders to write down each program method process. Below is an outline to help address each scenario followed by further explanation.

PROGRAM METHOD SAMPLE

Goal:

_____ -
_____
_____

Fatimoh Harris

Objective 1:

_____
_____

Objective 2:

_____
_____

When
_____
\# Who _____
Active Verb
_____

Measureable Quantity
_____

Targeted change/behavior/learning
_____

Task 1:
_____
_____

Task 2:
_____
_____

There may be additional tasks and goals associated with your plans.

Goals and _objectives_ DO NOT have the same definition.

Goals describe what your project/program intends to accomplish. It can be a general statement.

List a goal for your agency:

_____

_____

_____

Goal example: Our goal is *to improve reading levels of academically at-risk 3rd grade students* from John Paul Elementary School during the 2017/2018 school year.

Goals answer the question, *"What is the purpose of this plan, and what is it trying to achieve?"* Make sure the goals can be observed or measured for the evaluation and assessments.

S.M.A.R.T. objectives are measurable outcomes of the project/program that are **S**pecific or detailed, **M**easurable, **A**chievable activities, provide **R**esults and **T**ime-related. You will see the acronym **S.M.A.R.T.** often to help illustrate the definition of objectives.

Objectives show what will be *changed* **or** *learned* during program activities using *measurable processes*.

When writing objectives, your statement should also include the format that answers *when, who, an active verb, a measurable amount, and the change/activity clients will experience from the program.*

S.M.A.R.T. OBJECTIVES

S – Specific (or exact)

M – Measurable (quantifiable data and type of clients/service)

A – Achievable (realistic activities)

R – Result-oriented (show a change, improvement or maintained)

T –Time-related (length of services or timetable upon completion)

Objective example:

Harris Institute of Excellence after school academic program will improve reading levels of thirty, 3rd grade students, currently scoring state standardized reading levels below 2.0 after participating in our program nine months of the 2017/2018 school year.

Timeline example: A community center job training program may require the following timeline after the notice of funding award is received May 1, 2019 for the program to begin August 1, 2019. A brief sample of this timeline is listed below.

- Hire contractor to remodel classroom May 3, 2019 – May 10, 2019
- Equipment purchases May 7, 2019
- Hire instructor by July 1, 2019

Explain the objectives in the proposal writing

S – Who/what will this program/project target?

M - What targeted change/behavior or learning will take place?

A - Use realistic/obtainable measures.

R - What are the expected outcome(s) after participating in this program/project?

T - How long will it take to accomplish your plan after funding approval notification?

What objectives may be included in an after school celebration for student's grade progress?

Objective 1

_____

_____

Objective 2

_____

_____

Fatimoh Harris

Tasks are actions or steps needed to accomplish the goals set.

Tasks example: Purchase 12 bags of large balloons from Family Dollar on Tuesday for the celebration of the afterschool student's grade progress.

Tasks answer who or what, when needed, identify location/person, gives a measure quantity and target a change/behavior/learning.

When _____Tuesday_____

\# Who/What __Balloons_____

Active Verb __Purchase_____

Measureable Quantity ___12 Bags_____

Targeted change/behavior/learning: _To celebrate students success_

What other tasks may be included for this celebration?

Task 1:

_____

_____

Task 2:

_____

_____

ACTIVITY - Test Your Knowledge

Complete the below activity for a program from your agency. If you do not have an agency, create an activity for a health fair for men held 12 months from now.

Goal:

_____

_____

_____

Objective 1:

_____

_____

Objective 2:

_____

_____

      When

_____

    # Who _____

    Active Verb

_____

Measureable Quantity

_____

Targeted change/behavior/learning

_____

Task 1:

_____

_____

Task 2:

_____

_____

PROGRAM MEASUREMENTS: Assessments and Evaluations – Using proven methods that work

The program measurements section will show evidence researched through proven methods have been professionally tested through the assessment and evaluation processes. These processes should illustrate researched based proof that the concepts of the program design is capable to deliver services and produce the changes needed to help resolve or relieve the issues addressed in the problem/need statement.

The funder is not interested in donating money to a program/project with shaky proposal projections, unproven concepts and strong possibilities of failing. In other words, competence and confidence need to be demonstrated throughout the proposal.

How will grant makers know this project/program is effective? How will services be measured?

These questions are answered through findings in the evaluation. An evaluation is the analysis at the end of a program that exam how effective the program worked for the participants and within the community served. The agency purpose of existence is to make a positive impact in their service area. Evaluations are sometimes done in individual segments and through a compilation of various quantitative and qualitative assessment testings' used to demonstrate the program strategies articulate success.

The evaluation is directly tied to the objectives and goals and it defines the program's measurements of success. Grant makers seek measurements that have been professionally and/or academically tested through research conducted from universities, scientifically and through other professional industries. Peer reviewers may give high scores for evaluations measures that align with the grant makers purpose, demonstrate a clear plan and use proven methods.

Measuring the effectiveness of programs and operations is very important and can be performed using various quantitative and qualitative assessment resources such as surveys, tests, reports and interviews. Your agency should discuss how measurements the agency use will be tallied and explain how these measures will help improve areas of client needs in the program measurements proposal section.

- Quantitative evaluation uses *numeric or objective* information of an agency and/or client.

- Qualitative evaluation uses information from *behavior and attitudes* of an agency and/or client.

- Program assessment *measures the skill or behavior levels* of individuals or groups.

  o For example, a math tutoring program may measure math skills through a pre-test and post-test assessment. The results determine the program impact and success and the outcome(s) are systematically connected to the evaluation process.

Evaluations ANSWER the following questions:

1. How will the agency measure program/operational success?
2. How will the agency know when it has made a difference?
3. How often will the agency measurements be collected and what method will be used to collect them?
4. What changes/improvements will be made with approved grant funding?
5. Who will make the decisions for the changes from the evaluation findings?

Grant makers mission are to see the impact of positive accomplishments and gain return on investments as a result of their donation. This is why the processes for program measurements are included in building the operations of Nonprofit Administrations®. Strategy planning sessions from the agency stakeholders should discuss sound program design and outcomes, program measures (assessments and evaluations), research based program curriculums and sustainability plans which show viability for contributions identical to presenting a business plan to an investor to prove the agency will exist beyond the grant period. These processes are discussed in detail in our Nonprofit Administration® Workshops and *Starting & Starting: The Nonprofit Industry Handbook.*

Budgets

The purpose of the budget is to prove the financial plans have been established and the services identified in the proposal prove that resources of financial support are needed to operate. In other words, the budget justifies the program or operational needs discussed within the proposal. Grant makers want to see that you have thought through your anticipated expenses **and** have prioritized your request to only ask for what you need.

The budget is the line-by-line item listing of all revenue (income), including in-kind (freely donated products/services are considered as income/revenue) and expenses (resources to be paid out). Each program/service the agency provides should be included in the operations budget. For example if the agency provide a youth program, a senior program and a pet adoption program, the cost of each program should have separate budgets per program. It is best to breakdown the cost of each program in this way because the combined cost identifies the cost for the entire operating budget, minus in-direct administration cost.

The financial support from other contributors should be shown on the budget in the revenue area. This description of support can greatly strengthen the decision making process of grant makers for your agency.

Grant makers often require a written narration with the budget explaining cost associated with line item request. The budget is a compilation of operations, program and project cost of the service year. Depending on the type of grant being requested, for instance program, operational or a project, the budget will have to be broken down to fit the grant makers funding interest. For example, if the grant maker will only fund programs and only want the program budget, the agency should *only* submit the proposal and budget information that pertains to the program interest of the grant maker of which the agency is applying.

Do not submit a budget that is not requested by the grant maker. Remember each grant maker guidelines vary and your agency must remain flexible to *each* grant maker's individual request. A sample program budget can be found in the appendix.

OPERATING and PROGRAM BUDGET = TOTAL REVENUE and TOTAL EXPENSES

Strategies for budget planning are a part of the Nonprofit Administration® process and should be completed before the development/grant admin. process begin. An extensive nonprofit budget chapter, operating and program budget samples are provided in *Starting & Surviving: The Nonprofit Industry Handbook* by Fatimoh Harris and can be ordered at www.grants4me2.webs.com or call 219-810-4039.

Sustainability

Sustainability has increasingly become a major factor in grant maker's decisions to funding nonprofit agencies. It is a written plan that describes strategies to sustain the agency future existence beyond grants and should include income based strategies. Identifying the agency sustainability plan is becoming a common request by grant makers during the application process. It helps grant makers determine the agency's strength of existing if funding is awarded.

Just as bankers decide on financing for-profit entities based on their ability to pay back loans through self-sustaining income, grant makers identify with this strategy by measuring if the agency has the capacity to perform the proposed services after rewarded. They want to know if the agency's operational strategy plan have self-sustaining *income*-based plans. For example a book store *owned by the nonprofit agency* (not a board member or stake holder) is an example of self-sustaining income operating to help support the agency operations.

Grant makers may measure the capacity of the nonprofit administrators reviewing their past and current qualifications, the experiences of the board of directors and look for activities the agency conducts within the community or region it serves during their sustainability review. If the agency is a start-up, grant maker's may measure risk by reviewing the proposal, conducting site reviews, interviewing board members and staff and reviewing a full organizational strategy and sustainability plans. There are many professional resources such as Excel Professional Grant Writing & Nonprofit Services that can help your organization identify and prepare operational and sustainability plans. These planning processes should be completed and/or revised annually before the proposal process.

Appendixes

Appendixes are the section of the application where support material is provided. Supported material may consist of additional information requested by the grant maker such as previous year and current budgets, 501(c) (3) determination letter, IRS 990, letters of support or other material. Providing the requested materials in this section is very important. Missing items can result in a rejected funding request. Only include appendixes when grant makers request or allow additional information. Unsolicited material can also result in a funding rejection.

Reports

After funding is approved and usually at the end of the funding period, grant makers request a report from grantees that show how their contribution was used. Grant makers review funding reports to see how accurate the agency allocated donated funds as described in the agency's awarded proposal. Any issues should be immediately reported to the grant maker for resolve and resolution at the time the issue is identified.

How will you know when you have made a difference?

At what point of services performed can the agency say "we are succeeding"? Explain the details that lead to success. What impact do services make within the community and city? Tell a couple of before and after stories from clients that prove there are successes occurring through the agency programs. Talk about the continued success from clients in the stories six months after your agency helped them. Do not create fake stories of testimonies from clients when writing foundation proposals to increase opportunities for grant rewards.

How Will You Report?

Reporting demonstrates accountability and ethical practices to the board of directors, clients served, the general public, donors and grant makers. Because nonprofits are public entities, be expected to show funding investors and the public the agency IRS 990 and annual reports. Other benefits of reporting includes:

- Informing the community the agency services and accomplishments
- Announces donors/grant maker's philanthropic partnership
- Provide resourceful information to help other organizations

Grant makers want to be updated about their investment according to each grant maker's individual communication standards. In the proposal, mention the agency's openness to communicate with the grant maker and provide material required to strengthen the partnership.

ACTIVITY - Test Your Knowledge

List five evaluations questions grant makers want
answered when reading proposals.

1. _____

_____

2. _____

_____

3. _____

_____

4. _____

_____

5. _____

_____

Fill in the blanks

1. The _____ in the proposal is crucial in
its _____ to peer readers and other decision
makers.

2. The _____ _____ should be written
after the proposal is completed.

3. Place the proposal breakdown in sequential
order 1-9.

___ Executive Summary

___ Problem/need Statement

___ Program Design

___ Reporting

___ Budget

____ Program Measurements

____ Appendix

____ Cover letter/Letter of Intent

____ Grant Application

4. The sales piece for the proposal is the

_____ _____

5. The _____ _____ describes your agency's purpose or reason for existence and aligns with the agency's services provided to clients.

6. The _____ statement explains *why* your project/program is necessary for the target population the agency serves.

7. The _____ of your resources should be included in the _____ and _____ in the proposal.

8. Appendixes are the section of the application where _____ _____ is provided.

9. List various questions the proposal should answer for the problem/need statement.

- _____

_____

- _____

_____

- _____

_____

- _____

_____

- _____

_____

10. The _____ method/design actions identifies with the resources needed and required timeline for the success of the services provided.

11. Equipment, staff, money and partnerships are valuable _____ needed to operate the agency.

12. List the words for the acronym **S.M.A.R.T**. that relates to measurable outcomes for objectives.

S_____ M_____ A_____ R_____
   T_____

13. What are goals?

_____

_____

14. Give an example of a goal in a sentence.

_____

_____

15. What are objectives?

_____

_____

16. The _____ justifies all expenses and is consistent with the proposal narrative. It also adheres to the funders guidelines for request.

17. A _____ plan is a written plan that describes strategies to sustain the agency future existence beyond grants and should include income based strategies.

18. _____ evaluation uses _____ or
_____ information of an agency and/or
client.

19. _____ evaluation uses information from
_____ and _____ of an agency and/or
client.

PROGRAM MEASUREMENTS – Using proven methods that work

Use the below outline to practice identifying goals, objectives and tasks.

1. Write a goal, 2 objectives and 3 tasks for one of your programs/projects.

    Goal:

    _____

    _____

    _____

    _____

Objective 1:

_____

_____

_____

_____

Objective 2:

_____

_____

Fatimoh Harris

When

_____

\# Who _____

Active Verb

Measureable Quantity

Targeted change/behavior/learning

Task 1:

Task 2:

Task 3:

2. Besides grant writing, write a goal, 2
objectives and 5 tasks to help plan
sustainability strategies to help your agency
continue existing in the future. *Grants are
NOT sustainable plans.*

Goal:

_____

_____

_____

_____

Objective 1:

_____

_____

_____

_____

Objective 2:

_____

_____

_____

_____

When

_____

Who _____

Active Verb

_____

Measureable Quantity

_____

Targeted change/behavior/learning

_____

Task 1:

_____

_____

Fatimoh Harris

Task 2:

_____

_____

Task 3:

_____

_____

Task 4:

_____

_____

Task 5:

_____

_____

Chapter 8 WHO DECIDES HOW GRANTS ARE DISTRIBUTED?

Decision Makers

Final allocation decisions are made by the grant maker's allocation committees, trustees and board members. Peer/grant reviewers contribute to the decision making process as well. A peer/grant reviewer main duties consists of observing, reporting, and evaluating assigned agencies and programs with the goal of making objective assessments and funding recommendations according to the grantors review processes. Their responsibilities are as follows:

- Serve as the liaison between grant makers and assigned agencies.
- Conduct a comprehensive and aggressive examination of assigned agencies and programs/services by identifying issues, concerns and expectations.
- Read all written materials on assigned agencies.
- Monitor and record progress made by agencies in addressing issues/concerns raised by grantors.
- Attend site visits to assigned agencies.
- Show integrity through fairness and unbiased decision making skills.

- Report assigned findings and evaluation to other panel and chair members.
- Base all recommendations on grantors funding criteria and procedures.
- Participate in all decision making with other panel members and attend all meetings and trainings.

Grant Industry Tips

The following Grant Industry tips may be helpful:

o Ask for a copy of the scoring rubric to help construct a stronger proposal. A rubric sample is in appendix.

o Try to plan the operating and program budgets 12 months ahead of time. Planning eliminates rushed grant processes. Start the proposal process at least 12 months before the deadline. If changes are made to the process from the grant maker, your agency can then make proper adjustments early.

o Communicate true stories of testimonies from clients when writing foundation proposals.

o Use persuasive writing for foundation proposals.

o The annual report should include the following information:
- Mission statement of the agency
- Summary of the past year's program accomplishments
- List of all board members
- Financial data with the total income from the previous fiscal year, ending net assets, program expenses and fundraising and administrative categories with the same

information provided in the financial
statements

o Always package the application and proposal as directed
by the grant maker.

o Make the problem statement seem solvable with hope
for a solution.

o Use and cite up-to-date, relevant statistics and
information.

o Make sure the executive summary sale your request
because it will be the only portion some grant makers will use
to decide if they should read the proposal further.

o Follow the grant maker packaging instructions
COMPLETELY. Do **not** add anything extra to try to increase
your agency's funding chances. Unrequested additional
information will result in lower scores and can cause your
agency **not** to receive funding.

Grant Makers Scoring Rubrics

Following the instructions of the grant maker,
application guidelines and scoring rubric is the first step to
position your agency for grant rewards. Clearly explaining
each applicable area of the scoring rubric will help your
agency receive higher scores and the reviewer's
recommendation.

Please do not frustrate the readers or decision makers
by adding information not requested. *Unauthorized
material will not be read and can jeopardize the entire
request as an automatic rejection.*

Grant makers always have guidelines that are used by
reviewers and final decision makers to score proposals. The

rubric is a guideline that indicates how closely your agency followed directions to complete the proposal/application and how it aligns with funding requirements. Rubrics vary according to the requirements of the grant maker. The scores range according to the strength of each proposal section.

Your agency can request a copy of the reviewer's comments when a proposal request have been denied. It is best to use the information from the grant reviewer's comments to strengthen the proposal before resubmitting it the following funding cycle. Sometimes, if your agency completes the proposal process early, grant makers will critique the proposal and allow changes to be made before a final submit. This is *not* required by grant makers. It is based on their choice and time. An example of a grant maker's rubric can be found in the appendix.

ACTIVITY - Test Your Knowledge

True or False

1. A rubric is a guideline that indicates how closely your agency followed directions to complete the proposal, application and how it aligns with funding requirements.

____

2. Your agency can not request a copy of the grant reviewers comments when a proposal request has been denied. ____

3. Always package the application and proposal with additional material to help win the favor of grant makers.

____

4. Use argumentive, objective writing for foundation proposals. ____

5. Outdated statistics and information can still be a resource for the proposal. ____

6. Peer/grant reviewers do not contribute to the decision making process. ____

7. The annual reports should include a summary of the past year's accomplishments. ____

8. A site visit may be included in the grant reward process. ____

9. All rubrics are identical according to the interest or topic proposed. ____

10. Fake stories of testimonies from clients when writing foundation proposals should be created to increase opportunities for grant rewards. _____

Chapter 9 PROPOSAL ACCEPTANCE & REJECTION NOTIFICATION

Proposal Rejection

DON'T DESPAIR! Even the best grant writers receive reward rejections. Proposal rejection does not determine the end of your philanthropic world.

Grant Maker's Response
Rejections can simply be caused by one or more of the following:
- Funding interest did not align with grant maker
- Unclear expressions/narrations in proposal
- Too many agencies applied resulted in exhausted funding
- Requirements of the rfp guidelines not fully addressed
- Low grant/peer reviewer scores

Although any of the above will cause low scores from peer reviewers and rejections from grant makers, I do not agree with the emotional aspects of rejections due to these reasons being viewed as the absolute final decision of the grant maker. The Freedom of Information Act allow agencies to request review comments from government and foundation grant makers. The rejection letter usually includes contact information, and a grant tracking code may be included for federal notices.

Sometimes, especially with foundations and some state agencies, funding allocations remain with the grant maker which leaves the possibility of a decision review to disburse the grant maker's remanding funding. Agencies could qualify for cases such as these when peer review scorers are at the boarder of the qualifying status and the grant maker decide to give the agency an opportunity to advance or when an approved agency reject the grant reward.

Agency Responsibilities

Agencies have the responsibility of following proper guidelines and instructions of grant makers. This includes proper organizational preparation processes to avoid stress and wasted time of the Grant Administration® team or grant writer and wasting time of the agency. Below are tips to aid the agency during a proposal rejection:

- Make sure the agency and grant maker funding interest align
- When permissible, ask the grant maker questions that appears unclear. Do not assume responses.
- If grant maker's time is permissible, ask if they can review the proposal
- Use grant maker's and peer reviewer's critiques to improve the proposal
- Re-assess the proposal approach (requested amount, methods, grant maker's critiques, etc.) for the next funding cycle
- Create a grant calendar at least 12 months before the due date

- Demonstrate community support in the proposal and with support letters
- Make the proposal process a team effort
- Submit proposals earlier than the due date
- Build relationships with potential grant makers
- Invite grant makers to the agency for a site visit and/or events

The possibility of reward rejection is one of the main reasons to have a sustainability strategy or back-up plan that includes agency income-based strategies to avoid agency closure and budget deficits.

CONGRATULATIONS! *YOU'RE APPROVED!!*

A reward letter gives great satisfaction to the agency after the proposal process is completed. However, the complete steps for acceptance are not achieved with only the reward letter.

Now, the agency must adhere to the reward requirements such as, agree to terms of the grant maker to continue or begin payment arrangements, establish grant account(s), complete certifications and compliances and complete grant reports.

Working as partners with the grant makers will ensure a productive relationship. When an emergency occur within the agency such as financial crisis with programs unrelated to the reward, do not co-mingle finances with the expectations of replacing funds. If there is a surprise grant maker inspection, your agency will be liable for legal repercussions and the entire funded amount demanded to be returned. Your agency would not be allowed to participate in future funding request from the grant maker. Remember, grant makers communicate and have relations with other grant makers. Don't jeopardize the ethical principles of funding and those of the agency.

Preparing For A Site Visit

Site visits may be required before the grant reward or as a part of the reward agreement. It should be a welcoming experience to grant makers that display the pride of your organization. Inviting grant makers for a site visit during the letter of inquiry/intent stages is strongly suggested.

Site visits may be needed for a number of reasons such as helping the grant maker learn more about your agency, to legitimize agency services, to continue funded services, or as a quality control mechanism. The entire agency should be made aware of the site visit and staff/participants expectations should be aligned to present an organized, professional establishment.

Your inspection team should consist of all of the following: executive director, program director, board representative, collaborating partner(s), agency client(s) or as pre-designed in the grant maker site visit preparation check list. Preparation and processes should be a team effort.

To avoid the mystery behind the qualifications of a site visit, ask the grant maker if there is a check list or scoring device to better prepare the agency for passing the inspection.

If the grant maker does not have a specific inspection device, use the tips below to help leverage inspections with your team:

- Prepare the facility for a tour – designate a tour guide with positive enthusiasm
- Review the site visit announcement letter to help prepare for discussion with the grant

maker and to identify succession of the site visit

- Prepare talking points related to the grant makers interest
- Make sure administrative records and files are organized – be prepared for the grant maker to review them
- Be prepared to answer questions – review the submitted proposal or funding contracted
- Use short effective client demonstrations from the grant maker's program interest or from other programs if the visit is for a program that do not currently exist
- Practice the site visit plans before the actual visit – ensure participants know their roles
- Thoroughly clean the facility and if possible - fix facility repairs unrelated to the proposal request
- Be prepared to assist with the grant makers logistics such as ensuring collaborating partners preparation, grant makers travel arrangements and administrative processes

FINAL REFLECTIONS

Now that we have concluded the processes of Grant Administration®, it's time to take on the challenge of completing and **successfully** winning grant funding for your organization.

Let me know how successful my book have been in obtaining your agency grant rewards. Feel free to contact me for help at excelservices07@yahoo.com or 219-810-4039.

Thank you for purchasing my book.

Have GREAT SUCCESS!

Fatimoh Harris

STARTING & SURVIVING: THE NONPROFIT INDUSTRY HANDBOOK

Coming March 2017

This book focuses on engaging board members, administrators, staff and volunteers in day-to-day Nonprofit Administration® and management skillsets. It teaches the foundations needed to operate a productive nonprofit agency. Enlightened readers will learn strategy planning processes to organize, establish and transition nonprofit operations that effectively accomplish the agency's mission. Steps identified in this book lead to sustainable income and grant funding opportunities.

RESERVE YOUR COPY TODAY!!!

Topics

- ➤ **Nonprofit Administration®** – *The business behind the mission*
- ➤ **Nonprofit Start-up**
- ➤ **Standard Office Procedures**
- ➤ **Office Etiquettes**
- ➤ **Board Selection**
- ➤ **Recording Board Minutes**
- ➤ **Industry Updates**
- ➤ **Nonprofit Industry Glossary**
- ➤ **Board Governance**

Topics cont.

- **Planning Strategies**
  - o Goal vs. Issue Based Planning
  - o Capacity Building
  - o Operating
  - o Sustainability
  - o Programs and Services
- **Budget Preparation**
- **501(c)(3) Exemption**
- **Program Curriculum Models**
- **Measuring Success**
- **Effective Partnerships and Collaborations**
- **Marketing**
- **Fundraising**
- **Grant Readiness**

Bulk copies available at discount rates.

RESERVE YOUR COPY TODAY at Amazon, www.grants4me2.webs.com or excelservices07@yahoo.com

PRE-ORDER ONLY $7.99

APPENDIX

1. Test Your Knowledge Answers
2. Sample LOI
3. Sample Program Budget
4. Sample Grant/Peer Reviewer Score Rubric
5. Sample Grant/Peer Reviewer Score Guideline
6. Sample Logic Model
7. Research Tips - Grant Industry Data and Funding Resources
8. AFP Donor Bill of Rights
9. Grant Industry Glossary Terms
10. List of Excel Professional Grant Writing & Nonprofit Services

TEST YOUR KNOWLEDGE ANSWERS

Chapter 1

ACTIVITY - Test Your Knowledge

1. What is the definition of a grant?
   Answer: Grants are contributions donated from a grant maker/donor for exempt purposes

2. Do grants have to be repaid? If so, why or why not?
   Answer: Grants are NOT loans. They do not have to be repaid to the funder, but the agency must prove they will be ethically responsible and demonstrate financial accountability and have a sustainable future.

3. Is a social security number ever needed in the grant or nonprofit processes? If so, when?
   Answer: Social security numbers are never needed for grants or nonprofit start-up processes. Loans require personal credit identification such as social security numbers, some type of down payment and a repayment schedule.

Matching

1. e   2. d   3. c   4. a   5. h   6. b   7. f
8. g   9. j   10. i

Chapter 1 cont.

True or False

1. false   2. true   3. false   4. true
5. false   6. true   7. false
8. FALSE

Chapter 2

ACTIVITY - Test Your Knowledge

True or False

1. false 2. false 3. false 4. true 5. true

6. true 7. true

List three search tips that help discover your agency service needs.

Use the agency discretion

List five resources found from researching foundation books/website.

Use your agency discretion

Matching

1. e   2. c   3. i   4. k   5. d   6. g   7. a   8. j   9. h   10. f   11. b

Chapter 2 cont.

Write three fundraising strategies that can be used for your nonprofit.

Use your agency discretion

Answer the following:

Your state may require the agency to register with the attorney general office to solicit charitable contributions.

Chapter 3

ACTIVITY - Test Your Knowledge

1. Money, training, supplies and time are examples of resources.

2. Logic models are best used to help identify the effectiveness of outcomes/results and are used for evaluation purposes.

3. List three examples of your agency outputs: *Use your agency discretion*

4. Sustainability planning is an example of the agency planned work.

5. Purchasing equipment and supplies is an example of the agency inputs.

6. Short and long-term goals is an example of the agency outcomes.

Chapter 3 cont.

7. The content of logic models consists of two phases, the agency's <u>planned</u> <u>work</u> and the <u>intended</u> <u>results</u>.
8. Work plans consist of <u>processes</u> and <u>inputs</u>.
9. The agency's intended results consist of <u>outputs</u> and <u>outcomes</u>.
10. Describe two processes your agency will conduct. ***Use your agency discretion***

Chapter 4

ACTIVITY - Test Your Knowledge

1. List the terms for LOIs.

   <u>Letter of Intent</u>   <u>Letter of Inquiry</u>
   <u>Letter of Proposal</u>

2. What is a term for a letter of proposal?
   <u>mini grant</u>
3. The most common grant makers for LOI's are <u>foundations</u> and <u>corporations</u>.

True or False

1. Community for-profit businesses do not contribute to nonprofit agencies. <u>false</u>

Chapter 4 cont.

> 2. The problem statement can be excluded from the LOI. <u>false</u>
> 3. The entire operating budget should be included in <u>all</u> LOIs. <u>false</u>
> 4. The LOI can be signed by the program manager. <u>false</u>
> 5. The LOI is the initial sales pitch and introduction of your agency. <u>true</u>

Matching

> 1. b 2. c 3. a 4. g 5. f 6. d 7. e

Chapter 5

ACTIVITY - Test Your Knowledge

True or False
> **Communicating with Grant makers**
> 1. <u>false</u>
> 2. <u>False, unless the grant maker allows scheduled visits.</u>
> 3. <u>true</u>
> **Grant Applications**

> 1. Grant makers funding priorities define the *interest* your agency seeks to fund. <u>False, the agency mission and funding needs should pre-align with the grant maker.</u>

Chapter 5 cont.

2. All grant maker application deadlines are on rolling basis. <u>false</u>
3. It is best to begin working on grant proposals 3 months before deadlines are due. <u>false</u>
4. 501(c) (3) determinations are not required to complete online applications. <u>false</u>

Fill in the blanks

1. The White House Office of <u>Faith Based</u> and <u>Neighborhood Partnerships</u> is a resource for nonprofit agencies.
2. <u>Federal</u> applications can be found on the website grants.gov.
3. In order to include your agency application in a NOFA, your agency should contact your <u>state</u> office.
4. <u>Funding priorities</u> define the philanthropic interest grant makers seek to fund.
5. <u>Online applications</u> are commonly referred to as e-grant applications.
6. Funding is announced usually 30 to <u>45</u> days before the due date.
7. <u>Printed</u> and <u>online</u> applications can usually be found at the company, foundation or government agency website.

Chapter 6
ACTIVITY - Test Your Knowledge.

True or False

1. <u>false</u> 2. <u>false</u> 3. <u>true</u> 4. <u>true</u> 5. <u>true</u>

Fill in the blanks

1. Options of commitments received from MOU/collaborations can be in areas such as equipment usage, <u>location</u> usage, providing volunteers and <u>staff</u>, <u>financial</u> support or service exchanges.

2. The partners can serve in their areas of specialty, state <u>how</u> the collaboration work and <u>receive</u> an agreed <u>amount</u> of grant funding as needed per partner.

3. If your partners will participate in the grant being requested, the <u>MOU</u> should state <u>how the collaboration of activities</u> will be <u>managed</u> effectively and <u>which agency</u> has been selected as the <u>fiduciary agent</u> of the grant after rewarded.

4. Verification a proposal is received from the grant maker is the role of the <u>proposal writer.</u>

Chapter 6 cont.

5. Before formally agreeing to the partnership, there should be a <u>clear</u> <u>understanding</u> of how each partner will receive benefits.

Matching

1. b 2. d 3. e 4. a 5. c

Chapter 7
ACTIVITY - Test Your Knowledge

1. List five evaluations questions grant makers want answered when reading proposals.
    1. How will the agency measure program/operational success?
    2. How will the agency know when it has made a difference?
    3. How often will the agency measurements be collected and what method will be used to collect them?
    4. What changes/improvements will be made with approved grant funding?
    5. Who will make the decisions for the changes from the evaluation findings?

Fill in the blanks

1. The <u>information</u> in the proposal is crucial in its <u>deliverance</u> to peer readers and other decision makers.

2. The <u>executive summary</u> should be written after the proposal is completed.

Chapter 7 cont.

3. Place the proposal breakdown in sequential order 1-9.

   1. Cover letter/letter of intent (LOI)
   2. Grant application
   3. Executive summary
   4. Problem/need statement
   5. Program design – goals, objectives and program plans
   6. Program measurements
   7. Budget
   8. Appendix
   9. Reporting

4. The sales piece for the proposal is the <u>executive summary</u>.

5. The <u>mission statement</u> describes your agency's purpose or reason for existence and aligns with the agency's services provided to clients.

6. The <u>problem/need</u> statement explains <u>*why*</u> your project/program is necessary for the target population the agency serves.

7. The <u>cost</u> of your resources should be included in the <u>budget</u> and <u>discussed</u> in the proposal.

Chapter 7 cont.

8. Appendixes are the section of the application where <u>support material</u> is provided.

9. List various questions the proposal should answer for the problem/need statement.
   - Who are the beneficiaries? How are they benefitted?
   - What is the nature of the problem?
   - How did your organization realize the problems exist?
   - What is currently being done about the problem within the community/state?
   - What alternatives remain available after funding has been exhausted?
   - What will happen to your project/program if the agency is not funded by the funder?
   - How will problems be solved?

10. The <u>program</u> method/design actions identifies with the resources needed and required timeline for the success of the services provided.

11. Equipment, staff, money and partnerships are valuable <u>resources</u> needed to operate the agency.

Chapter 7 cont.

12. List the words for the acronym S.M.A.R.T. that relates to measurable outcomes for objectives.

    <u>Specific</u> <u>Measurable</u> <u>Achievable</u> <u>Result-oriented</u> <u>Time-related</u>

13. What are goals?
    Goals describe what the project/program intends to accomplish. It can be a general statement.

14. Give an example of a goal in a sentence.
    Use your agency discretion

15. What are objectives?
    Objectives are measurable outcomes of the project/program. Objectives show what will be changed or learned during program activities using measurable processes.

16. The <u>budget</u> justifies all expenses and is consistent with the proposal narrative. It also adheres to the funders guidelines for the request.

17. The <u>sustainability</u> plan is a written plan that describes strategies to sustain the agency future existence beyond grants and should include income based strategies.

Chapter 7 cont.

18. <u>Quantitative</u> evaluation uses <u>numeric or objective</u> information of an agency and/or client.

19. <u>Qualitative</u> evaluation uses information from <u>behavior and attitudes</u> of an agency and/or client.

Use the below outline to practice identifying goals, objectives and tasks.

1. Write a goal, 2 objectives and 3 tasks for one of your programs/projects.
   Use your agency discretion

2. Besides grant writing, write a goal, 2 objectives and 5 tasks to help plan sustainability strategies to help your agency continue existing in the future. *Grants are NOT sustainable plans.*
   Use your agency discretion

Chapter 8

ACTIVITY - Test Your Knowledge

True or False

1. <u>true</u> 2. <u>false</u> 3. <u>false</u> 4. <u>false</u> 5. <u>false</u>
6. <u>false</u> 7. <u>true</u> 8. <u>true</u> 9. <u>false</u> 10. <u>false</u>

LETTER OF INQUIRY SAMPLE

We Love Animals, Inc.
445 Main Street
Chicago, Illinois
312-555-5555
Weloveanimals.org
weloveanimals@dogscats.com
Mr. Willie Harris, President

May 10, 2017

Attn: Ms. Gwendolyn Freeman, Grant Director
Apple Jacks Foundation Corporate Giving
123 Forest Lane
Chicago, IL 60603

Dear Ms. Freeman:

We Love Animals, Inc. is writing to Apple Jacks Foundation to request $10,000 in program support for our Pet Adoption Program for Dogs and Cats during your May, 2018 funding cycle. We Love Animals have been in existence for 25 years and self-sufficient without grant support until the increase of rescues in 2016. We have very strong internal control policies which have helped us sustain thus far. We are in need of your assistance to help purchase dog and cat supplies such as food, safe handling equipment and

Fatimoh Harris

help with veterinarian cost to keep our animals healthy.

In support of your field of interest of animal rescues for dogs and cats, our adoption program will help resolve the problem of unsafe conditions for displaced strays in the city. According to Chicago Animal Shelter 2015 main drop off site report, there has been a 37% increase in the number of stray dogs and cats picked up by their center rescuers compared to 29% during 2014. Also, our center rescue workers reports a combined 43% increase of rescued stray dogs and cats during 2016 compared to 34% in 2015. Unfortunately, this rise in numbers will continue to place dogs and cats in danger unless communities join forces together to help them become safely adoptive.

Ms. Gwendolyn Freeman
May 10, 2017
Page three.

Our program staff and partners consist of an experienced program manager trained in Illinois Animal Safety Practices (IASP), seven licensed pet rescuers, partnership with Chicago Animal Shelter and Cook County Animal Patrol. Our partners work with our mission of saving the lives of dogs and cats by dropping off dogs and cats at our location when their shelters are full. While they are at our center the rescue workers then clean and deliver them to our local veterinarian were they receive a health exam and shots.

Since established, we have rescued 32,805 animals and placed 27,017 in safe homes. Our annual operating budget is $230,000. However, our Pet Adoption Program for Dogs and Cats budget is $25,000. We have also requested $3,000 from the Edward James Animal Fund and are awaiting notification by June 30, 2017. A 2% portion of our store sales is allocated to this program. A cost summary is as follow:

Ms. Gwendolyn Freeman
May 10, 2017
Page four.

Personnel	$8,500
Non-personnel	$2,200
Indirect	$2,280
Direct	$12,020
TOTAL	$25,000

Our revenue streams consist of fundraising, pet sales from our store, engraved pet memorial stones and sales from our programs. Your help is greatly needed to continue serving our animal friends and helping to create families.

Thank you for considering our agency and a full proposal will be submitted upon request. We welcome you to a site visit and to review our evaluation plan, 990, list of board of directors and 501c3 letter. Please feel free to contact me at 312-555-5555.

Sincerely,

Mr. Willie Harris, President

SAMPLE PROGRAM BUDGET

SUPPORT AND REVENUE	Projected	Committed
Cash Contributions		
Fundraising Campaign	$15,000	$15,000
Grants		
United Way	$35,000	$35,000
Foundations	$20,000	$ 13,500
In-Kind Contributions		
Donated equipment	$ 1,000	$ 1,000
Volunteers		
General labors	$ 3,000	$ 3,000
Earned Income		
Program fees	$22,940	$18,250
Product Sales	$ 5,700	$ 5,700
Total Support & Revenue	**$102,640**	**$91,450**

EXPENSES	Total	Grant Request
Personnel Expenses		
Program Manager		
1 @ $27,500 year	$27,500	$ 6,500
Instructor – part time		
1 @ $15,000 each	$15,000	
Tutors – part time		
2 @$4,500 each	$ 9,000	
Subtotal	**$51,500**	
Fringe benefits & taxes 20%	$10,300	
Total Personnel Expenses	**$61,800**	**$ 6,500**

SAMPLE PROGRAM BUDGET cont.

EXPENSES	Total	Grant Request
Non-Personnel Expenses		
Occupancy (rent/utilities)	$10,500	$4,690
Supplies	$ 800	
Equipment	$ 2,500	
Telephones	$ 700	
Curriculum material	$ 10,500	
Postage	$ 325	
Professional dues	$ 1,000	
Insurance	$ 500	
Maintenance & repairs	$ 1,500	
Staff training	$ 1,600	
Professional fees	$ 1,200	
In-kind labor	$ 3,000	
Total Non-Personnel Expenses	**$34,125**	**$4,690**
Total Direct Expense	**$95,925**	**$11,190**

(Direct cost means all cost associated with a program/activity i.e. toys or books) (calculate total personnel expense (61,800) + total non-personnel expenses (34,125)) = 95,925 Total Direct Expense

Indirect
Program Expense 7%   **$6,715**
(Indirect cost is cost not directly associated with a program/activity i.e. agency security workers) (calculate direct program expense 95,925 x 7%) = 6,714.75 (rounded to 6,715) Program Expense

Total Program Expense   **$102,640**
(Calculate total direct expense (95,925) + indirect program expense (6,715)) = 102,640 Total Prg Exp

SAMPLE GRANT/PEER REVIEWER SCORE RUBRIC

Below you will find short excerpts of scoring rubrics from various grant makers.

The table below outlines the overall criteria used in the scoring and evaluation process for the two steps included in the application review. Corresponding weights are included where applicable.

STEP 1: APPLICATION SUSTAINABILITY SCREENING RELATIVE WEIGHT

Does the applicant describe a sustainable project?

Are the included budget information and financial claims made credible and verifiable?

Are the reductions/reallocations (if present) permanent? 25 points

STEP 2: APPLICATION REVIEW APPLICANT INFORMATION

Does the applicant have experience with projects similar in size and scope and/or demonstrate capacity through partnerships to carry out the proposed project? 5 points

SAMPLE GRANT/PEER REVIEWER SCORE RUBRIC cont.

PROJECT DESCRIPTION

Does the applicant present a strong argument for the innovative concept that achieves the stated fund goals?   35 points

IMPLEMENTATION

Has the applicant presented an outline of a thoughtful implementation plan, including contingencies for mid-course correction? 20 points

SUBSTANTIAL IMPACT AND LASTING VALUE

Does the application demonstrate substantial value and lasting impact by providing information which includes relevant background research, opportunities for replication, a statement of impact and a plan for evaluating impact through quantifiable results? 40 points

SAMPLE GRANT/PEER
REVIEWER SCORE RUBRIC cont.

Category	Point Value	Required Elements	Score
E. Financial Stability	5	Description of organization's annual budget and funding sources.	
		Explanation of organization's internal controls and accountability procedures.	
		Documentation of audit or other similar report included in appendix.	
		Criteria / Rationale	
	0	The applicant has major omission of required information about the organization's financial stability. No financial audit or applicable report is included in	

		the appendix.	
	3	The applicant has provided a general description about the organization's budget and financial controls but important details are lacking. The financial audit or applicable report is included in the Appendix but may not be complete.	
	5	The applicant has provided a clear and comprehensive description of the organization's budget and funding sources. The organization has strong internal controls and accountability procedures in place. The organization provided a financial audit or applicable report to demonstrate the organization's fiscal stability.	

Comments (Financial Stability):

SAMPLE GRANT/PEER REVIEWER SCORE GUIDELINE

Below you will find short excerpts of guidelines from various grant makers.

PROCESS FOR STEP 1: SUSTAINABILITY REVIEW

Applications will undergo an initial screening by three separate scorers to ensure that the proposal includes an explanation of how the project will be self-sustaining. If the project will result in increased, ongoing spending, the applicant shall show how the spending will be offset by verifiable, credible and permanent spending reductions.

This stage of the screening involves a fiscal review of application responses and budget documents to ensure that the description of the budget, the project proposal and potential project impact demonstrate sustainability. The screening also will determine whether reductions/reallocations (if proposed) are permanent and that the claims made in the application are verifiable and credible. Based on the scores of the three grant scorers, grant advisors will evaluate and make a determination of whether a proposal has demonstrated sustainability (see Scoring Process) and will recommend to the Governing Board if the applications should be

SAMPLE GRANT/PEER REVIEWER SCORE GUIDELINE cont.

rejected (not sustainable) or undergo further review (sustainable) in step two of the process. **Any project that has not met the criteria of a verifiable, credible plan for sustainability will be rejected and not be reviewed in step two of the process.**

Criteria
Fiscal scorers and screening evaluation will focus the scoring on how well the application responses and budget documentation meet the following criteria:

- Illustrate a concept that is sustainable with ongoing costs offset by verifiable, credible and permanent spending reductions.

Using the financial documentation and the answers provided in the sustainability section (questions 13-17) of the application, scorers will score items on a yes/no scale to determine the likelihood of sustainability. The assigned score will be based on the overall strength of the answer and evidence provided.

SAMPLE GRANT/PEER REVIEWER SCORE GUIDELINE cont.

Criteria

The overall Criteria for the XYZ Fund application review are listed below. Scorers will determine how well the responses:

- Propose a strong argument for an innovative concept that represents bold and visionary thinking.
- Outline a thoughtful implementation plan;
- Proposes the thoughtful description of quantifiable results of the project that can be benchmarked;
- Demonstrate substantial value and lasting impact.

Each answer will be rated on a scale that moves from vague/unclear/lacking innovation to strong evidence/exemplary/highly innovative. The assigned score will be based on the overall strength of the answer and evidence provided.

SAMPLE GRANT/PEER REVIEWER SCORE GUIDELINE cont.

READ all proposals through (before scoring) to get a feel for the proposals individually and in comparison to each other (relative to readability and complexity only).

EVALUATE the quality of EACH response in EACH proposal, at the beginning of the scoring process by considering the following. Is the response:
• Relevant and responsive to the criteria?
• Comprehensive and well thought-out?
• An effective, logical, and realistic approach to the problem?

Comments (feedback) justify each score!
  • If there are questions about scoring, reviewers' comments should be sufficient to defend the scores without further explanation.
  • Write comments that clearly explain, to anyone reading them, why a particular score was given.
  • Comments should be constructive versus critical, professional, helpful, and impartial.

SEQUENCE OF LOGIC MODELS

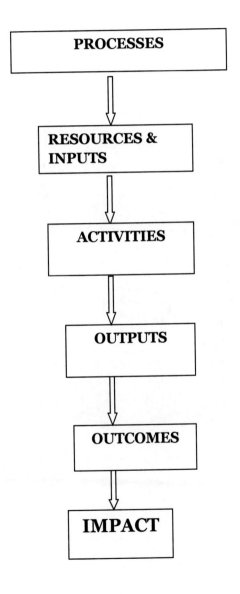

SAMPLE PROGRAM LOGIC MODEL

Englewood Community (EC) Food Pantry

Resources	Activities	Measurable outputs	Short-term & intermediate outcomes (6 – 12 months)	Long-term outcomes (2-5 years)	Program Goals
➢ Partners/ Collaborators: * Harris Food Bank *EC Board Members & Ministry * Chicago Foundation * Anchorage Grocer's *Jewel Foods *Local Businesses * Community * Local pantries	➢ Continue to engage partnership with food bank by attending meetings and receiving instructions to serve community	➢ Establish an organized food pantry partnership with food bank in Chicago	➢ Continue working with food bank to prepare for partnership and continue discussions of building pantry network	➢ Increase intake capacity to assist disadvantaged households of 5 low-income multi-apartment complexes of over 300 households and home owners in area	➢ Reduce City of Chicago and Englewood Community hunger rate
	➢ Work with food bank and other pantries to build alliance to strengthen operations	➢ 24 Distributions yearly, 2x per month	➢ Monthly meetings with food bank and local pantries to build collaborative alliance and discuss strategies to reduce hunger in Englewood Community	➢ Clients utilize other City of Chicago and Englewood Community Services	➢ Engage in impactful partnerships that strengthen self-sufficiency for struggling Englewood Community households
	➢ Build relations with community, local businesses and other grantors to solicit donations/resources	➢ Increase services from 75 to a minimum of 125 disadvantaged households to have access to free food by May	➢ Include Herman Raster Elementary School students in food bank weekend backpack program	➢ Strengthen collaborative efforts with pantry partners by engaging in MOU to help eliminate abusing pantry services and help agencies obtain new clients.	➢ Provide pantry resources for disadvantaged households
EC p/t paid staff & volunteers * Coordinator * Registration Clerk	➢ Attend trainings from food bank for effective operations	➢ Distribute 50,000 pounds of food	➢ Raise awareness of EC and other local community service partners		
➢	➢ Purchase/monitor equipment/supplies for services ➢ Hire licensed pest control for bi-weekly inspections	➢ Create opportunity for other EC community services and programs (i.e. youth and adult education/recreational nutrition, finance management classes)			

RESEARCH TIPS - GRANT INDUSTRY DATA AND FUNDING RESOURCES

GRANT INDUSTRY DATA

usaspending.gov and federalarchives.gov – post quarterly grant awards and contracts

schoolgrants.org – K-12 grant information

factfinder.census.gov – demographics and economic statistics

foundationcenter.org – RFP notifications and industry information

federalregister.gov – current and past funding notifications

grants.gov – grant information for more than 900 grant programs

cfda.gov – Catalog of Federal Domestic Assistance is a federal data archive site of federal grant programs and cooperative agreements

fedstats.gov – post statistics for all federal agencies

omb.gov – The Office of Management and Business publishes the White House regulations for federal awards

bea.gov – Bureau of Economic Analysis has regional data

Local data and funding is available from city and state departments, federal departments, foundations, corporations and local small businesses. Also, ask questions from other community agencies and partners.

DONATED RESOURCES
Gifts and Kind International - giftsandkind.org
Gifts in Kind provides nonprofit organizations access to donated products and special pricing programs. There are some fees involved with receiving donations and services. This organization also accepts donations.   (SOME FEES APPLY)

National Association for the Exchange of Industrial Resources - naeir.org
NAEIR offers access to donated materials to organizations that provide care for the ill, needy, or minors. The products may be used to further an organization's mission and in its everyday operations. NAEIR accepts donations.   (SOME FEES APPLY)

GOVERNMENT GRANTS & RESOURCES

One of the goals of the Office of Faith-Based and Neighborhood Partnerships is to make sure that community organizations are aware of grant opportunities that may be relevant to them throughout the Federal Government. Neither the office nor the agency centers administer or manage federal grant programs. However, the links to grants below can help you identify those grant opportunities where faith-based and neighborhood organizations are being engaged as partners throughout the Federal Government.

Grants.gov - This electronic system allows you to search for grant opportunities across multiple factors such as agency, services, populations, and those most recently announced.

USASpending.gov - This electronic system allows you to identify grants that have been awarded to entities in your community.

Recovery.gov - The website includes information about federal grant awards and contracts as well as formula grant allocations.

Grants.gov (grants.gov/applicants-recovery) - This website within Grants.gov lists information about grant opportunities related to the American Recovery and Reinvestment Act or ARRA.

Fatimoh Harris

GOVERNMENT GRANTS & RESOURCES
continued

Research and Resources Database
(transparency.cit.nih.gov/fbci)- This searchable database
provides an opportunity to quickly and easily find
information based on keywords or categories associated
with the work of faith-based and community organizations.

**Corporation for National and Community Service
Resource Center** (nationalserviceresources.org) - The
Resource Center is the knowledge management training
and technical assistance that is the best source for
connecting service programs with targeted training and
information.

**Department of Health and Human Services Tools and
Resources Page** (hhs.gov/fbci/tools & resources)- This
White House site provides tools and resources that have
been assembled to enhance the work of faith-based and
community organizations in areas such as technical
assistance, emergency preparedness, research, and more.

GOVERNMENT GRANTS & RESOURCES
continued

Incorporate Your Nonprofit Organization in Your State
(usa.gov/business/nonprofit_state)- Many states have
online information about nonprofit organizations and
charitable activities.

Federal Tax Information for Charities and Nonprofits
(irs.gov/charities)- This website provides information about
points of intersection between organizations and the IRS.
The content includes explanatory information, and links to
forms that an organization may need to file with the IRS.

Source: Retrieved from
http://www.whitehouse.gov/administration/eop/ofbnp/resources January/2015

FEDERAL GRANTS
Centers for Faith-based & Neighborhood
Partnerships Departments

**White House Office of Faith-based and Neighborhood
Partnerships**
Melissa Rogers, Executive Director
Email: whpartnerships@who.eop.gov
Website: www.whitehouse.gov/administration/eop/ofbnp

**Center at the U.S. Department of Health and Human
Services (HHS)**
Phone: (202) 358-3595
Email: partnerships@hhs.gov
Website: http://www.hhs.gov/partnerships

FEDERAL GRANTS Cont.
Centers for Faith-based & Neighborhood Partnerships Departments

Center at the U.S. Department of Commerce
Phone: (202) 482-3928
Email: jdickson@doc.gov
Website: http://www.commerce.gov/office-secretary/center-faith-based-and-neighborhood-partnerships

Center at the U.S. Department of Housing and Urban Development (HUD)
Phone: (202) 708-2404
Email: partnerships@hud.gov
Website: http://www.hud.gov/offices/fbci

Center at the U.S. Department of State
Phone: (202) 647-3137
Email: fbci@state.gov
Website: www.state.gov/s/fbci

Center at the U.S. Department of Veterans Affairs (VA)
Phone: (202) 461-7689
Email: vapartnerships@va.gov
Website: http://www1.va.gov/cfbnpartnerships/

Center at the U.S. Department of Agriculture
Phone: (202) 720-2032
Email: collaborate@usda.gov
Website: http://www.usda.gov/partnerships

FEDERAL GRANTS Cont.
Centers for Faith-based & Neighborhood Partnerships Departments

Center at the U.S. Department of Homeland Security (DHS)
Phone: (202) 646-3487
Email: infofbci@dhs.gov
Website: http://www.dhs.gov/fbci

Center at the U.S. Agency for International Development (USAID)
Phone: (202) 712-4080
Email: fbci@usaid.gov
Website: http://www.usaid.gov/partnership-opportunities/faith-based-community-organizations

Center at the U.S. Department of Education
Phone: (202) 401-1876
Email: edpartners@ed.gov
Website: http://www.ed.gov/edpartners

Center at the Small Business Administration
Phone: (202) 205-6677
Email: partnerships@sba.gov
Website: http://www.sba.gov/fbci

FEDERAL GRANTS Cont.
Centers for Faith-based & Neighborhood Partnerships Departments

Center at the U.S. Department of Labor
Phone: (202) 693-6017
Email: CFBNP@dol.gov
Website: http://www.dol.gov/cfbnp

Center at the U.S. Department of Justice
Phone: (202) 305-7462
Email: partnerships@ojp.usdoj.gov
Website: http://ojp.gov/fbnp/

Center at the Environmental Protection Agency
Phone: (202) 564-4308
Email: partnerships@epa.gov
Website: http://www.epa.gov/fbnpartnerships

Point of Contact at the Corporation for National and Community Service
Phone: (202) 606-7554
Email: fbnp@cns.gov
Website: http://www.nationalservice.gov/for_organizations
/faith/index.asp

Source: Retrieved from
http://www.whitehouse.gov/administration/eop/ofbnp/offices/federal
January/2015

LOCAL GRANTS

Grants to assist small and growing nonprofits of all sizes can be sought at your local community foundations and businesses, municipalities, city and state departments. Research and resources for local and nationwide grant makers can be found at your local library.

DONOR BILL OF RIGHTS

PHILANTHROPY is based on voluntary action for the common good. It is a tradition of giving and sharing that is primary to the quality of life. To assure that philanthropy merits the respect and trust of the general public, and that donors and prospective donors can have full confidence in the not-for-profit organizations and causes they are asked to support, we declare that all donors have these rights:

I. To be informed of the organization's mission, of the way the organization intends to use donated resources, and of its capacity to use donations effectively for their intended purposes.

II. To be informed of the identity of those serving on the organization's governing board, and to expect the board to exercise prudent judgment in its stewardship responsibilities.

III. To have access to the organization's most recent financial statements.

IV. To be assured their gifts will be used for the purposes for which they were given.

V. To receive appropriate acknowledgement and recognition.

DONOR BILL OF RIGHTS
cont.

VI.   To be assured that information about their donations is handled with respect and with confidentiality to the extent provided by law.

VII.   To expect that all relationships with individuals representing organizations of interest to the donor will be professional in nature.

VIII.   To be informed whether those seeking donations are volunteers, employees of the organization or hired solicitors.

IX.   To have the opportunity for their names to be deleted from mailing lists that an organization may intend to share.

X.   To feel free to ask questions when making a donation and to receive prompt, truthful and forthright answers.

Endorsed by

- Independent Sector
- National Catholic Development Conference (NCDC)
- National Committee on Planned Giving (NCPG)
- Council for Resource Development (CRD)
- United Way of America

Grant Industry Glossary

1. **Acquisition Cost** – the entire cost to acquire assets to be used for operational purposes
2. **Allocate** – a common industry term that means *to distribute*
3. **Approach** – a term that describe how goals and activities are reached
4. **Award Letter** – a commitment letter from grant makers for funding awards
5. **Beneficiary** - d*onee* or *grantee* receiving funds from the grant maker/donor
6. **Bequest** – the donation after a donor's death
7. **Brick and Mortar** – a capital funding term used for remodeling and construction
8. **Capacity Building or Technical Assistance** – Fundable assistance for operational or management purposes. It can also include assistance for fundraising, budgeting, grant/technical writing, financial planning, strategic planning, program planning, board development, training, legal advice, marketing, consulting and other management needs.
9. **Carryover** – remaining year end program funds that may or may not be used for the following year

Grant Industry Glossary cont.

10. **Catalog of Federal Assistance (CFDA)** – federal data archive site of federal grant programs and cooperative agreements
11. **Challenge/Matching Grant** – Grants that stimulate support from other donors because they are contributed only when the grantee is able to raise funds from other source(s).
12. **Commitment Letter** – indicates from the funder or partnering agency what will be received during the grant cycle
13. **Competitive Grant** – competitive unrestricted grants
14. **Cost-Benefit Analysis** – the process of comparing expenses to objectives that analyze the effectiveness of cost to operate
15. **Cost Sharing** – portion of cost shared by the agency partners for the purpose of achieving a common goal
16. **Data Universal Numbering System (DUNS)** – a Dun and Bradstreet numbering system that is used to identify organizations
17. **Declining/Graduated Grant** – multiyear grants that reduce in payouts annually
18. **Deficit** – the amount needed to meet the expenses of the budget

Grant Industry Glossary cont.

19.**Demonstration Grant** – a grant based on the model of a new program that can be duplicated based on documented effectiveness of the program

20.**Depreciation** – the process of allocating the use of fixed assets during its expenditure period

21.**Development Department** (See Grant Administration®)

22.**Direct Cost** – direct expenses specifically related to program/services/projects such as staff, equipment and curriculum

23.**Direct Mail** – solicitation through mass mailings

24.**Discretionary Grant** – federal government or foundation competitive grants

25.**Donor** - The individual or organization that donates the grant or contribution.

26.**Donor Bill of Rights** – The Association of Fundraising Professionals (AFP) guidelines for donors that demonstrate ethical operational practices of nonprofits.

27.**Donor Designated Funds** – a fund setup by a donor with specific terms for distributions

Grant Industry Glossary cont.

28. **E-Business Point of Contact (E-Biz POC)** – person responsible for Grant Administration® and management
29. **E-Grant** – online electronic grant application
30. **Earmark Grant** – a grant written into legislation by Congress
31. **Empowerment Zone/Enterprise Community** – areas designated by state or federal governments to receive priority funding for economic development
32. **Endowment** - permanent funds invested into nonprofits to provide continued income support
33. **Evaluation** – the analysis of a program that exam how effective the program is in the community or its' industry impact
34. **Evidence Based Program Design** – the process of implementing proven research to program design

Grant Industry Glossary cont.

35. **Exempt Operating Foundation** – A private operating foundation that is publicly supported for ten tax years or existed since 1983, consisting of less than 25% disqualified persons and without a disqualified person during its tax year (irs.gov).

36. **Fiduciary or Fiscal Agent** – lead agency responsible for managing the grant reward of a partnership or collaboration

37. **Goals** – Goals describe what the project/program intends to accomplish. It can be a general statement.

38. **Grant** – contributions donated from a grant maker or donor for charitable purposes

39. **Grant Administration®** – also referred to as the duties of the Development Administration/Department, describes the summary of work performed to successfully meet the funding needs of a nonprofit and/or for-profit business applying for grant support. The Grant Administration® team processes applications, completes paperwork, provides grant management and perform duties to maintain or increase sustainable funding for nonprofits and/or for-profit entities.

Grant Industry Glossary cont.

40. **Grant Consultant** – a professional contracted to provide consulting services in Grant Administration® duties

41. **Grant Maker** – A grant making organization or funder that creates grant opportunities for nonprofits in exchange of making contributions according to the interest of the grant maker.

42. **Grant Manager** – a person who manages grants received to avoid fraudulent practices for an agency

43. **Grant Reporting** – a report to funders stating how compliance and requirements were achieved by the grantee

44. **Grant Writer** – a person who writes grant proposals, complete RFP applications and letters to receive funding for an organization

45. **Grantee/Donee** – grant or donation recipient

46. **In-Direct Costs** – cost that support general or administrative operations

47. **In-Kind Contributions** - contributions such as equipment, products, professional and labor volunteers, meeting space, or other property received instead of cash donations

Grant Industry Glossary cont.

48. **Impact** - defines how your agency improved administratively, within the communities served, and strategic processes over time and at the end of funding and operating periods

49. **Intangible Property** – assets of stocks, trademarks, patents, copyrights and goodwill

50. **Letter of Inquiry (LOI)** –The initial contact for many grant makers by way of a brief letter describing the nonprofit activities and funding request. The LOI helps the grant maker decide if a full proposal will be required according the matching interest of the grant maker and requesting agency.

51. **Letter of Intent** – A letter that informs grant makers of the agency intent to request funding. This process also helps grant makers prepare for the number of proposals they will receive.

52. **Letter of Interest** – is cross referenced with letter of inquiry definition

53. **Letter of Proposal** – another term for Letter of Inquiry but for some grant makers it can represent a full proposal of seven pages or less for small funding request.

Grant Industry Glossary cont.

54. **Letter of Support** – A letter written in behalf of an agency from supporting organizations or individuals to funders/grant makers.
55. **Loaned Talent** – an executive or skilled laborer given permission from their company to assist nonprofits in their area of expertise to improve operations
56. **Logic Model** – A theory or assumption process that connect short and long term outcomes with program activities/processes and theoretical assumptions/principles of the program.
57. **Measureable** – objectives and outcomes must prove quantifiable
58. **Memorandum of Understanding** – an exchange of services formally agreed between two or more partnering agencies that benefit the community/clients
59. **Merit Review** – a review scored based on a portion of the proposal

Grant Industry Glossary cont.

60. **Method** – process to achieve the objective

61. **Needs Assessment** – determining what activities need to be initiated or expanded to satisfy a situation

62. **NOFA** – Notification of Funding Availability in the *Federal Register* publication

63. **Objectives** –Objectives show what will be changed or learned during activities using measurable outcomes.

64. **Operating Cost** – the entire cost of operating a nonprofit or for-profit business

65. **Operating Income** – profit an agency or business generate without grants or donations

66. **Outcome** – the impact produced from client participation with your agency

67. **PA** – public announcement about funding available

68. **Peer Reviewer/Grant Reviewer** – a professional who participates in decision making processes for grant makers

69. **Performance Goal** – relates to objectives being specific, measurable, achievable, realistic and time related (S.M.A.R.T.)

Grant Industry Glossary cont.

70. **Personal Property** – moveable property that is not real property

71. **Planned Gift** – a gift that involves a lifetime giving plan from estate and personal contributions

72. **Pro Bono** – volunteer work donated free of charge by professionals

73. **Problem Statement** (Need Statement) – Presents the facts and evidence that support the need/problem for the project/program in your community/state. It establishes your organization understanding of the problem or need.

74. **Program**- occur ongoing or on a continuous schedule such as an after school program held throughout the school year

75. **Program Assessment** – measures skill or behavior levels of individuals or groups

76. **Program Cost** – cost associated with operating a program

77. **Program Income** – gross profits from program activities

Grant Industry Glossary cont.

78. **Program Method** – the action plan/processes of goals, objectives and tasks

79. **Project-** A project does not occur on an on-going schedule. A project can be an annual event like a back to school event.

80. **Proposal -** A grant proposal is a financial/in-kind request to enter partnership with donors/grant makers for the success of a common philanthropic goal. It narratives a proposed program/service in alignment of the agency's and grant maker's mission.

81. **Qualitative** – An evaluation that use information from behavior and attitudes of an agency and/or client.

82. **Quantitative** – An evaluation that use numeric or objective information of an agency and/or client.

83. **RFP** (request for proposal) – A notification of funding available from a grant maker for new or existing grants.

84. **Real Property** – permanent property that cannot be moved such as land

Grant Industry Glossary cont.

85. **Report/Final Report** – provides information to grant makers about how funding was spent and how effectively the program proposed was evaluated

86. **Rubric** – A guideline used by peer/grant reviewers to score proposals. It indicates how closely agency applicants followed directions of the rfp to complete the proposal, application and the alignment with funding requirements.

87. **Seed Money** – start-up or expansion capital used for operating cost

88. **Subjective Review** – foundations and corporations review process to determine grant reward recipients

89. **Surplus** – the amount remaining from the budget after all expenses are allocated

90. **Sustainability Plan** – A written plan that describes strategies to sustain the agency future existence beyond grants and should include income based strategies.

91. **Technical Assistance** – see capacity building

92. **Technical Meeting/Bidder's Conference** – A meeting or webinar held by the grant maker to give additional information about the funding opportunity.

EXCEL PROFESSIONAL GRANT WRITING & NONPROFIT SERVICES, LLC
P.O. Box 208
Griffith, IN 46319
(219) 810-4039   grants4me2.webs.com
Excelservices07@yahoo.com
Certified Women's Minority Business Entity (WMBE)
Fatimoh Harris, President & Certified Grant Writer®

Our Experience and Dedication
Excel has over 10 years of Nonprofit & Grants Industry experience, over $10 million in successful funding experiences by consultants and 98% of 501(c) 3 applications are IRS approved.

Essential functions of Excel are to conduct open and effective consultation with board members, staff and community partners, provide updated Nonprofit/Grant Industry strategies, research grant opportunities for current and future programs, prepare efficient documentation substantiating funding needs, write and coordinate winning proposals, maintain accurate grants/nonprofit database and monitor fundable programs according to each client Grant Administration® and Nonprofit Administration® needs.

Strategic methodologies we utilize are:
- Grant Administration®
- Nonprofit Administration®
- Strategic Planning
- Donor Development
- Board Governance
- Grant Research
- Organizational Management
- Proposal Writing
- Editing Services
- Budget Preparation
- Fundraising
- Nonprofit & Grant Workshop Training
- 501(c) 3 Preparation
- Transition Management
- Leadership Development

Strategic methodologies continued

Excel offer a range of services to help clients make informed decisions about managing their business activities. We help develop and implement a customized action plan to direct clients in paths that successfully work for them. We adapt a wealth of resources to help develop our client's business opportunities.

We have experience leading small and large-scale organizational change efforts. Excel provides one-on-one coaching sessions with key members of your agency to ensure ongoing focus, accountability and support to implement your organization plans. Excel recognize when changes are needed to produce the effectiveness of an organization and work diligently with your organization to fulfill your goals. Care is taken to create strong client/consultant partnerships that utilize best practices to focus on creating dynamic strategies to achieve client-centered results.

Our clients receive **personalized, confidential advice** and **implementation services** characterized by the highest levels of integrity, expertise and objectivity.

OUR MISSION

Excel specializes in helping nonprofit organizations and individuals, fulfill their charitable aspirations by increasing the impact of their philanthropic endeavors. Our goals are to enhance nonprofit organizations impact, financial sustainability of operations, create freestanding mission-centered agencies, and form mutually-beneficial relationships with funders. **We focus on capacity building strategies that promote organizational effectiveness.**

OUR VISION

Our vision is to help nonprofits carry out the key steps in developing mission-related opportunities using practical and cost-effective methods for their organization. We help clients build Nonprofit Management capacity by enhancing Nonprofit Administration®, and Grant Administration® efforts.

ABOUT THE AUTHOR

Ms. Fatimoh Harris, President of Excel Professional Grant Writing & Nonprofit Services and Excel Professional Services, is a successful Certified Grant Writer®, Nonprofit and For-Profit Corporate Consultant, Federal and State WMBE Certified Small Business Owner, Grant Reviewer, College Adjunct Instructor, Grant Administration® Instructor, Nonprofit Administration® Instructor, Workshop Facilitator and Author. Ms. Harris is the author of Navigating the Grant Industry® Handbook and Starting & Surviving: The Nonprofit Industry Handbook. She is also a member of American Grant Writers' Association and BoardSource.

Fatimoh Harris

Ms. Harris has over 17 years of professional administrative experiences including working with teams handling annual multi-million dollar budgets. She has successfully won over $3,000,000 in grassroots funding and 98% of 501(c) 3 applications are IRS approved for clients.

Ms. Harris is a native of Chicago, Illinois and has strong roots in the Christian and Social Service Communities. She works closely with nonprofit corporate leaders, board members, and teams applying excellence and ethical principles to satisfy their business needs. She is an experienced government and community Grant Reviewer who participates in Grant Administration® duties with teams that reward millions in grant funding to nonprofit agencies, *just like yours*.

Ms. Harris has proven executive decision making experiences to help your agency achieve financial success and impart strategies that will bring your agency mission to life.

OUR MOTTO:

Excellence is the result of caring more than others
think is wise, (Daniel 6:3)
Risking more than others think is safe, (Joshua 21:45)
Dreaming more than others think is practical, (Habakkuk 2:2-3)
and
Expecting more than others think is possible. (Hebrew 11:1)